Contents

P9-EES-317

Introduction

There is a great wealth of fascinating wildlife to be seen along the shore, and this book is designed for all those who, on vacation by the ocean or simply walking on the beach, want to identify and find out more about the animal or plant they have found. You find a shell washed up on the beach: is it an oyster, a scallop or a clam? Are you sure that plant on the shore or in shallow water really is a plant and not an animal like an anemone or a coral?

Seashore life is immensely varied and representative species from each major group have been included to enable the reader to identify a wide range of plants and animals.

How to use this book

The book is divided into nine sections covering plant and animal life, according to the general appearance of the species. These are **Plants**; **Plant-like Animals**; **Soft-bodied Animals**; **Animals with hard shells or bony plates**; **Animals with jointed legs**; **Shore Fish**; **Marine Reptiles**; **Seabirds** and **Marine Mammals**. Each section is identified by a different color band at the top of the page. In the main, these sections follow the recognized biological groupings, but many seashore species are so thoroughly adapted to their environment that they bear little resemblance to their closest relatives: Sea Slugs, for example, are gastropods and related to snails, but are soft-bodied with no shells. We have, therefore, added symbols representing the major biological groups of plants and animals, to aid identification and to place the species in context one with the other (see Fig. 1.)

The ability of different species to withstand the rigors of the seashore environment varies considerably. When you find an animal or a plant that you want to identify, try to note its exact position on the shore. Is it at high, mid or low tide level? Is it on or under rocks, in a pool, in sand, mud or gravel? To help you, each page carries this additional information: a shore "map" of the type or types of beach each species inhabits (see Fig. 2,) and, in the top color band, the tide level at which each species is most likely to be found (see Fig. 3.)

Guide to identification

First decide to which section your specimen belongs.

Plants Algae, which are marine seaweeds and encrustations, plants which form a close covering over the substrate on which they grow (like moss,) or flowering plants (most grow on land, but some are truly marine.)   **14–29**

Plant-like animals Gritty or slimy encrustations, fern-like, stony or flower-like, retracting when touched. If it is difficult to decide whether you are looking at a plant or an animal, place it in water: if it moves, it's an animal.   **30–38**

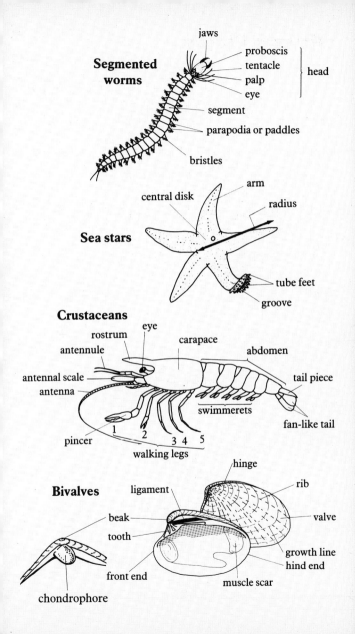

Segmented worms

jaws
proboscis
tentacle
palp
eye
head
segment
parapodia or paddles
bristles

Sea stars

arm
radius
central disk
tube feet
groove

Crustaceans

rostrum
eye
carapace
abdomen
antennule
antennal scale
antenna
tail piece
swimmerets
fan-like tail
pincer
1
2
3 4 5
walking legs

Bivalves

hinge
ligament
rib
beak
valve
tooth
growth line
hind end
front end
muscle scar
chondrophore

AN INSTANT GUIDE TO

SEASHORE LIFE

The plants and animals of
the North American seashore
described and illustrated in full color

Cecilia Fitzsimons

BONANZA BOOKS
New York

CAUTION

The ocean is beautiful and fascinating, but it can be dangerous and should always be approached with caution and respect. When exploring at low tide, never let the incoming tide cut off your route back to the shore. Watch out for large waves which can sweep the unwary off slippery rocks. Always keep a close eye on young children when they are near water.

© 1989 Atlantis Publications Ltd

This 1989 edition published by Bonanza Books, distributed by Crown Publishers, Inc., 225 Park Avenue South, New York, New York 10003.

Printed in Spain

ISBN 0–517–69111–6

h g f e d c b a

Soft-bodied animals A wide range of (mostly) small animals. They may have skeletal structures deep within their body, but none are visible on the surface.   **39–57**

Animals with hard shells or bony plates Primarily the molluscs, with cone spiral shells (gastropods,) or two-piece clam shells (bivalves.) Also included are echinoderms (urchins and sea stars,) with skeletons formed from bony plates in the skin. The related Sea Cucumbers are soft-bodied and grouped with other soft-bodied animals. Barnacles and tubeworms also secrete hard chalky plates and tubes.   **58–88**

The symbols below will identify the biological group of your species within each section.

Fig. 1 Key to animal and plant groups

 Algae Green, brown or red simple plants. Often leathery or slimy.

 Flowering plants, including grasses.

 Sponges Vase-like, encrusting or branching, many pores.

 Tunicates Vase-like or encrusting, two pores. Internal organs visible.

 Bryozoa Encrusting or mat-like colonies.

 Coelentrates Soft anemone-like body, contractile tentacles round mouth.

 Simple worms Unsegmented. Long and thin (nemerteans) or leaf-like flatworms.

 Segmented worms (Annelids) body with bristles, gills and/or tentacles.

 Molluscs Calcified shell and head, muscular foot. Varied shell shapes.

 Echinoderms Bony plates and spines embedded in the skin. 5 rows of tube feet.

 Crustaceans External skeleton, Jointed legs, may have pincers.

 Other Arthropods Insects, with 3 pairs of legs, and sea spiders, with 4 pairs.

 Fish

 Reptiles

 Birds

 Mammals

Animals with jointed legs (the Arthropods) with a tough or hard external skeleton, articulated by movable joints; they include shrimps, crabs and insects. Barnacles have jointed legs, but their shell is the more obvious feature so they are included above. **89–107**

Shore fish Fish easily seen on or from the shore. **108–112**

Marine reptiles Ocean-going turtles which come ashore to lay their eggs. **113**

Seabirds Birds commonly seen on or near the coast. **114–118**

Marine mammals Those species most readily seen from the shore. **119–121**

Habitat symbols and tidal levels

The habitat and tidal level in which a species normally lives can be quite specific and knowing them can be helpful in identification. The following symbols appear on each page:

Fig. 2 Key to habitats

 Rocks, stones & other hard substrates,

 Gravel

Sand

Mud

Open sea

When a particular species is found in more than one habitat, a combination of these symbols in the shore "map" identifies them.

Making a positive identification

Turn to the relevant pages and compare the illustrations and entries until you have identified your species. To help you confirm your identification, the size of the plant or animal is given at the top of the page. Unless otherwise stated, this figure refers to the maximum overall length, but should be treated with caution since only individuals living in optimum conditions reach maximum proportions; many will be smaller.

What's on a page

There are 4 boxes of text on each page giving different items of information:

Box 1 describes the distinguishing features of the plant or animal; this information, together with the illustration, will positively identify each species. **Box 2** completes the description and provides further details on biology, habits and other points of interest. **Box 3** describes where the species is found, its favored habitat, tidal level and geographical distribution around the coasts of North America. (State abbreviations on page 125.) Lookalikes, or similar species with which the featured species might be confused, as well as related, or other common species are included in **Box 4**; many of these are also illustrated, either as featured species themselves or on the "Other Species" pages in each section.

For a glossary of terms, see the endpapers.

Specimen page

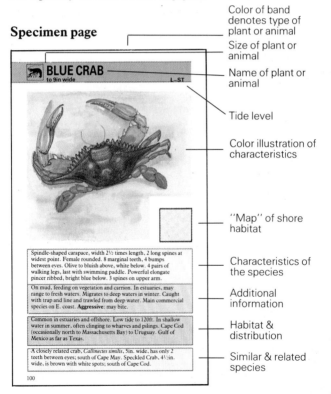

Color of band denotes type of plant or animal

Size of plant or animal

Name of plant or animal

Tide level

Color illustration of characteristics

"Map" of shore habitat

Characteristics of the species

Additional information

Habitat & distribution

Similar & related species

BLUE CRAB
to 9in wide
L–ST

Spindle-shaped carapace, width 2½ times length, 2 long spines at widest point. Female rounded. 8 marginal teeth, 4 bumps between eyes. Olive to bluish above, white below. 4 pairs of walking legs, last with swimming paddle. Powerful elongate pincer ribbed, bright blue below. 3 spines on upper arm.

On mud, feeding on vegetation and carrion. In estuaries, may range to fresh waters. Migrates to deep waters in winter. Caught with trap and line and trawled from deep water. Main commercial species on E. coast. **Aggressive**: may bite.

Common in estuaries and offshore. Low tide to 120ft. In shallow water in summer, often clinging to wharves and pilings. Cape Cod (occasionally north to Massachusetts Bay) to Uruguay. Gulf of Mexico as far as Texas.

A closely related crab, *Callinectes similis*, 5in. wide, has only 2 teeth between eyes; south of Cape May. Speckled Crab, 4½in. wide, is brown with white spots; south of Cape Cod.

100

11

Exploring the seashore

This book is designed to fit into your pocket or purse, so take it with you on your next vacation or visit to the coast. This way you can use it to identify plants and animals in their natural habitat on the shore without endangering them: on many beaches, overcollecting has seriously depleted populations. Many animals are found under weeds, rocks and boulders: **be sure always to turn rocks back to their original position** so that the creatures beneath will not die of exposure to sun, air and predators.

Tidal levels and zonation

The tidal cycle has two roughly equal highs and lows every 24 hours, with each day's tides about one hour later than the previous day's. Spring tides are the highest and lowest and occur every two weeks near full or new moon. The least extreme, or neap, tides occur in the intervening period. The best time to explore the shore is one hour before low tide, preferably at low spring tide. Go immediately to the water's edge and work your way back up the beach as the tide returns. Daily tide information is published in local newspapers.

Different plants and animals live at various levels of the shore (see Fig. 4;) those with least tolerance to exposure to air, sun, and temperature and salinity changes are found at the lowest levels, nearest to the sea. More tolerant species live near the tops of rocks or higher up the beach. Some can tolerate heavy wave action; others cannot and live in crevices, on the lee side of rocks, or only occur in sheltered bays and sounds. Deep rock pools often contain subtidal species.

Fig. 3 Key to tide levels

SZ **Splash Zone.** Margin of shore and land, but still affected by salt spray.

U **Upper shore.** The area above the average (mean) high tide level (MHW,) the upper limit of which is marked by the extreme highwater mark. Only covered by spring high tides and spray (EHWS.)

M **Middle shore.** The extensive region between the average high tide level and the average (mean) low tide level (MLW.) Typical shore conditions, being submerged by tide and exposed to air twice daily.

L **Lower Shore.** The area below the average low tide level (MLW) as far as the extreme low water mark (MLWS.) Only uncovered by spring low tides.

ST **Subtidal Zone.** Shallow waters; organisms living here are not uncovered but are still affected by changes in temperature and salinity not experienced in the open sea.

Fig. 4 Tidal levels and zonation

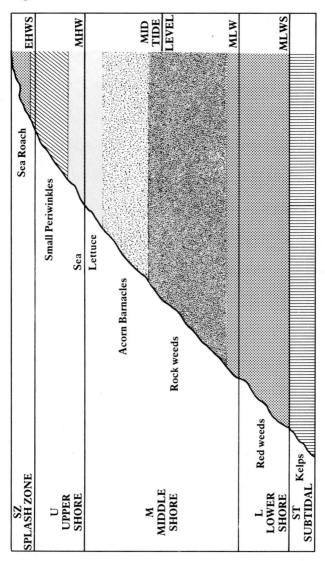

A soft lettuce-like weed. Pale translucent green. Older fronds are darker green and may have a white margin. Irregularly lobe-shaped with a small basal stalk.

Forms lettuce-like bunches, attached to the substrate by a short stalk. Abundant in summer, especially where fresh water occurs, in streams, runoffs, etc.

Grows on stones and rocks on upper, middle and lower shore. Also in shallow waters and rock pools, sandy bays and harbors. Often floats free and may be washed up. Atlantic and Pacific coasts.

Several species of **Enteromorpha** resemble Sea Lettuce in color and texture, but all have long tubular fronds.

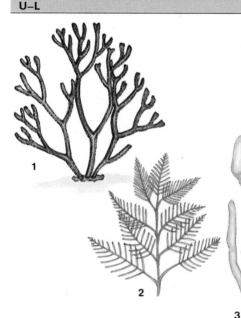

Sea Staghorn (**1**) 16in. long.
Dark green, bushy, branching,
with regular Y-shaped forks.
Branches cylindrical, ⅓in. wide
& spongy. Bleach yellowish.
Mid-low tide level & in shallow
water. Rocky shores, bays &
harbors, often anchored to
pebbles & shells. Alas.–Mex.,
N.J.–C. Cod.

Moss Weed (**2**) 4in. Several very
similar species, light or dark
green, bushy, regularly
branching to form fine, fern-like
clumps. Collapses out of water.
Mid-low tide, often in tidal
pools, protected waters. Fla.–
N.S. & W. coast.

Enteromorpha (**3**) 1ft. Bright
green like **Sea Lettuce**, but
long, narrow (1in.) hollow tubes,
several growing together. May
contain bubbles of gas. Tolerate
brackish water & pollution. May
rapidly cover mud flats. Bleach
white when dead. Upper shore,
pools & freshwater seepage.
Arc.–Carolinas & Pacific coast.

15

🌿 BLADDER WRACK
to 3ft

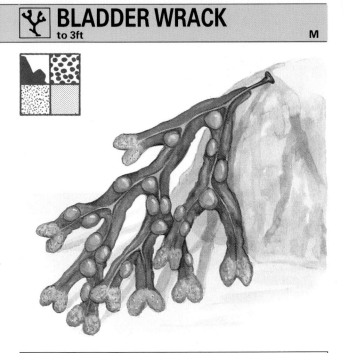

Regularly branched, flattened fronds with thickened midrib and (usually) paired air bladders. Olive green to brownish, drying to black. Stalk-like stipe expanded into basal holdfast which firmly attaches plant to rock. Reproductive bodies (receptacles) at frond tips are swollen, spongy and yellowish.

Rockweeds (*Fucus spp.*) are common worldwide in temperate seas. Form dense cover over rocks and other hard substrates. Shelter many plants and animals when the tide is out from the effects of heat and dessication.

On virtually any hard substrate on the middle shore. Exposed rocks, bays, salt marshes, or free-floating; wharves and pilings. Arctic to North Carolina.

Other species of *Fucus* are very similar, but have no air bladders. All are variable depending on the ecological conditions to which they are subjected.

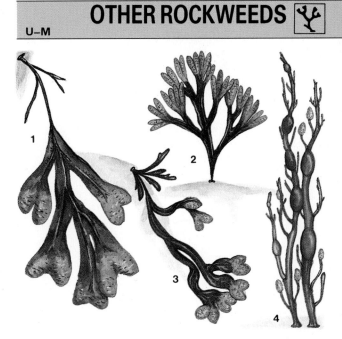

Western Rockweed (**1**) 4–20in. long. Flattened fronds with thickened midrib, olive, greenish brown to blackish as it dries. Yellowish, swollen, spongy receptacles at frond tips. On rocks & pilings, middle shore. Alas.–Cal.

Little Rockweed (**2**) Short, 2½–6in. Light brown, regularly branched fronds flattened but fairly thick & fleshy. Receptacles yellowish. Higher levels on exposed coasts. Forms a band with & above (**1.**) B.C.–C. Cal.

Spiral Rockweed (**3**) 6–16in. Flattened fronds with midrib, usually twisted near tips. No air bladders. Receptacles rounded with marginal ridge. On rocks, upper shore, usually above **Bladderwrack**. Nfld.–L.I. Not in very exposed areas.

Knotted Wrack (**4**) Very long stems (2ft. or more,) leathery olive green drying to green-black. Ribless stems, round near holdfast, becoming flatter, have egg-shaped air bladders & smaller golden yellow receptacles on side shoots. Prefer sheltered water, may cover some rocky estuarine shores. Not on exposed beaches. Mid shore, Arc.–L.I.

17

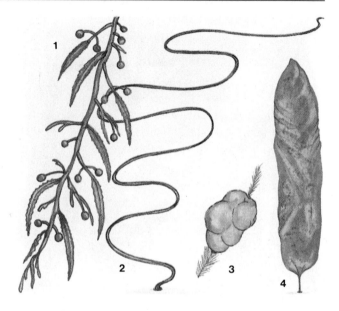

Gulfweed (*Sargassum*) (**1**) Stems at least 2ft. long have leaf-like spotted fronds with toothed margin & midrib, stalk bears pea-like ¼in. air bladders. Golden brown. Attached to rocks, lower shore & below. C. Cod Carib. Free-floating species without spotted fronds cast ashore in N.C. may carry exotic animals from Sargasso Sea.

Cord Weed (**2**) Whip-like, to 15ft. Olive-brown, slimy, hollow, floats. Attached by disk-like holdfast to stones & shells. Low tide & below, often on gravel. L.I.–Arc.

Sea Potato (**3**) 3–4in. Yellow-brown, globular or irregular mass. Thick-walled, rubbery, solid when young & becoming hollow with age. Grow on other seaweeds or on rocks. Lower shore. Nfld.–L.I., less common to N. Carolina.

Ribbon Weed (**4**) Large thin ribbon-like frond often over 1ft. long. Olive-brown to yellowish frond tapers sharply into basal stalk. Grows on rocks, stones & other seaweeds. Mid-low tide. Gulf of St. Lawrence–S. New Jersey.

Long, oar-like, golden brown blade with no midrib, smooth, ruffled at the edges or crumpled all over. Relatively thin stalk terminates in a two-layered root-like holdfast, firmly attached to the substrate.

Frond renewed each year by growth from top of stalk. Variable form: in summer blade is thin with ruffled edges, in winter thick and strap-like. Once used as a source of potash and iodine. Edible.

In tidal pools and attached to rocks, stones and shells. Extreme low tide to 60ft., especially in sheltered positions. Alaska to Coos Bay, Oregon; Arctic to north Massachusetts.

Common Southern Kelp: to 10ft. long. May be same species, certainly very closely related and similar in appearance. Long Island Sound to Gulf of Maine, locally to the Arctic.

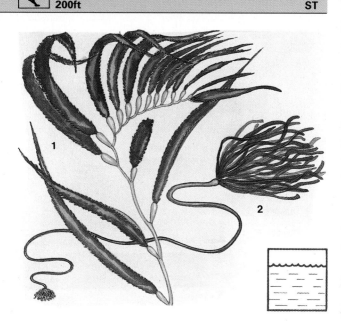

The repeatedly branched main stalk bears long leaf-like blades up to 15in. long. Each blade rises from a spherical float which is attached to the main stalk by a short stem. Massive holdfast either creeping rhizome-like or conical.

Largest kelps, often over 200ft. long. Harvested for algin, which is used in drug, food and other biochemical industries. Relies on large **Sea Otter** population to control Sea Urchins which eat young plants.

Subtidal to 250ft. in sheltered open seas. 2 closely related species: ***Macrocystis integrifolia*** (**1**) with creeping holdfast in shallower waters and tidal channels; *M. pyrifera* has conical holdfast, forms floating beds in waters 18–200ft. Alas. to Cal.

Bull Kelp (**2**:) 100ft.; 4–6in. round float bears many strap-like blades several feet long. Float connected to massive holdfast by flexible 40ft. hollow stipe. Pools, subtidal. Alas. to Cal.

Winged Kelps (**1**) 6–10ft.
Several very similar, possibly
interrelated species. Long,
strap-like blade with prominent
midrib, often frayed. Olive to
dark brown. Short, solid stalk
bears 2 rows of narrow
reproductive fronds. Edible.
Low tide & below; moderately
exposed coasts. Alas.–C. Cal.;
Arc.–C. Cod.

Ribbed Kelp (**2**) 3ft. long.
Brown strap-like blade has 5
parallel ribs down length. Small
root-like holdfast. Low tide &
below. West coast, California.

Sea Palm (**3**) 20in. tall. Like a
small palm tree. Thick stalk has
up to 100 strap-like blades (10in.
long) growing from top.
Attached to mid tidal rocks
exposed to direct surf. B. Col.–
C. Cal.

Horsetail Kelp (**4**) 3½ft. long.
Thick, rounded, flexible stalk
bears a broad shiny blade which
divides as it grows into many (6–
30) strap-like fingers. Brown.
On exposed rocks on extreme
low shore & down to 18ft. Arc.–
L.I.

21

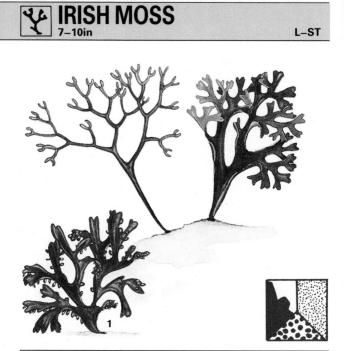

Flattened frond, repeatedly rounded forks form a single short stalk, but variable: may be long and narrow or short with broad fronds. Deep red, with bluish green iridescence under water. Green to yellowish in hot weather. Holdfast is a disk. Longer, narrow form grows in exposed sites.

In optimum conditions, forms a zone of vegetation between midshore rockweeds and low tide kelps. Edible and the source of the gel carrageenin, used in the pharmaceutical and food industries.

Attached to stones and rocks on all shores except mud. Often in tidal pools. Lower shore and below. Labrador to Long Island Sound.

Other red seaweeds usually have less rounded forks. **Tufted Red Weed (1:)** 3in. Purplish fronds curled at edges, covered with short bumps. Forms turf on rocks with Irish Moss. Nfld.–R.I.

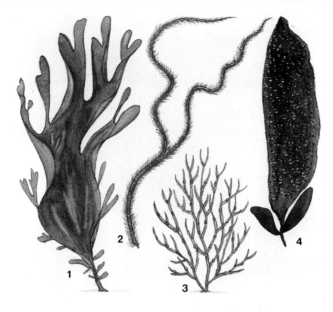

Dulse (**1**) To 1ft. Frond expands gradually from holdfast disk to form flattened branched fan. Deep purplish red, ribless, tough & rubbery. Older parts may bear smaller marginal leaflets. Edible & harvested in N.E. On rocks & kelp stipes, mid shore to shallow water. Arctic–Long Island Sound.

Chenille Weed (**2**) 2ft. or more. Long, thin, flexible fronds, occasionally branching & covered in fine, short leaflets which give a furry appearance. Nova Scotia–Tropics. In shallow waters, often washed ashore in bays & inlets.

False Agardhiella (**3**) 1ft. Stringy, coarse, bushy with irregular cylindrical branches. Reddish, brown or yellowish. Covered in wart-like reproductive protruberances. Mid shore, on rocks or partly buried in sand. Common south of Cape Cod & on Californian beaches.

Sea Tongue Algae (**4**) To 20in. or more. Several species with long, broad blade covered with tiny bumps like a Turkish towel. Deep red. Lower shore. B. Col.–Cal.

CORAL WEED
1–5in

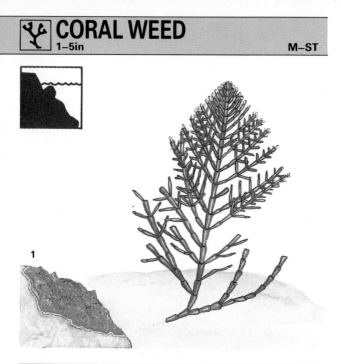

1

Plant consists of elongate, calcified segments, linked by pliable joints to form the frond. Main stem with branches, branchlets and their subdivisions exactly opposite. Purplish to red, pink or yellow with white tips. Holdfast encrusting.

A chalky mineral layer (calcium carbonate and magnesium carbonate) is deposited on the surface of the plant. Feels stiff and gritty to the touch. Bleaches white when dried.

On rocks, often forming a dense carpet, especially in tidal pools. Middle shore to subtidal. Newfoundland to Long Island; Alaska to Mexico.

Lithophyllum (**1**) is an encrusting coralline algae forming irregular, pink to violet, stony crusts. On rocks in pools; lower shore and below. Entire east and west coasts.

24

Long, narrow, flat leaves, ¼–½in. wide, grow up to 3ft. long from stems creeping beneath the sediment. Bright green leaves have evenly spaced parallel veins. Inconspicuous flowers and seeds, grass-like.

Flowering plants related to certain pond weeds, help to stabilize acres of soft sediment in bays and estuaries. Primary food of **Brant** geese in winter, also provide food and habitat for many other plants and animals, including turtles.

On mud, gravel and muddy sand; middle shore to subtidal in bays, sounds, and other protected waters. Arctic to South Carolina; Alaska to Mexico.

Surf Grass has leaves to 6ft. long, but narrow (³⁄₁₆–³⁄₈in.) On exposed rocks at and below low tide mark. Thinner leaved (⅛in.) species in pools, deeper channels. Both Alas. to Mex.

Evergreen shrub or, in tropics, tree. Green yellowish, lance-shaped leaves 2–4in. long. Shiny above, gray-green with fine hairs below. Leaves scattered with salt crystals. Tiny flowers (⅜in.) have 4 white petals. Fruit is a flat, rounded, 1¼in. capsule. Knee roots grow out from trunk and down into mud.

On south Florida, Gulf and Caribbean coasts, salt marshes and mud flats are replaced with mangrove swamps which support a rich and varied plant and animal life. Tangled aerial roots prevent waterlogging and stabilize the swamp.

Muddy shores, salt and brackish water. In mangrove forests. North and south Florida, Gulf coast to Texas, Mexico to Brazil and Peru; Bermuda and West Indies.

3 other species in southern Florida are tropical and less hardy. Red Mangrove closest to water's edge has aerial roots hanging from lower branches.

Coarse, scratchy leaves are stiff, gray-green, and usually rolled inward. Dense, cylindrical flower spike 4–8in. long, ½in. spikelets with fine hairs inside. Long creeping underground stems.

Introduced from Europe and planted extensively to stabilize dunes. Leaves roll up to conserve water, so are able to withstand dry conditions for long periods of time.

Once established, forms extensive banks on foredunes. On east and western coasts.

American Dune Grass similar, flowering spike less dense. Sea Oats have 16in. long, drooping leaves, and golden brown spikelets on 7ft. tall stems. Virginia to Florida and Texas.

Beach Morning Glory (1)
Flower 1½–2½in. wide, pink,
funnel-shaped, growing in leaf
axils & similar to Field
Bindweed. Thick, fleshy,
kidney-shaped leaves. Trailing
stems rise from deep rootstock.
Common on upper beach sands.
B. Col.–S. Cal. Flowers April–
September.

Sea Rocket (2) Flower ¼in.
wide, 4 small lavender petals.
Low, branching plant, 16–20in.
tall, with fleshy leaves, 3–5in.
long, lanceolate, wavy toothed.
Flowers July–September. High
on beaches. Lab.–Fla.; locally
around Great Lakes; entire
Pacific coast.

Beach Primrose (3) Flower ½–
1¼in. wide, 4 rounded yellow
petals. Leafy 2–4ft. stems trail
across sand from central rosette
of ovate leaves, ½–2in., covered
in gray hairs. Flowers April–
August. Upper beach sands. S.
Ore.–Baja Cal.

Silky Beach Pea (4) Pink &
white pea flowers, ¾in., in
dense cluster. 2–10 broad,
lanceolate leaflets, ¼–¾in.
long, grayish with silky hairs.
Flowers April–June. Sand
dunes. Wash.–C. Cal.

Slender Glasswort (**1**) 6–18in. high. Fleshy stems, usually much branched, opposite. Appears leafless, leaves reduced to scales. Flowers minute, at water's edge in salt marshes. Edible. N.B. & N.S.–Ga. Locally in Mich., Wis., Ill.

Salt Marsh Club Flower (**2**) ¾in.-long flowers pinkish & white, hidden in leafy calyx, pale yellow upper lip & 4-toothed lower. Hairy lanceolate leaves to 1in. Flowers May–September. Salt marshes. Nfld.–Fla. & Tex.

Sea Lavender (**3**) 1–2ft. high. Flowers ⅛in., 5 petals, pale purple in clusters along 1 side of stem. Leaves 2–10in., lanceolate, broadest towards apex, margins smooth or wavy. Flowers July–October. Abundant on tops of marshes. Nfld.–Fla. & Tex.

Salt Marsh Aster (**4**) 1–2ft. tall. Few flower heads of many white-pale purple ray flowers, ½–1in. wide. Weak, sparse leaves are fleshy & narrow, 6in. long. Flowers August–October. Often in masses on salt & brackish marsh tops. N.H.–Fla. & Miss.

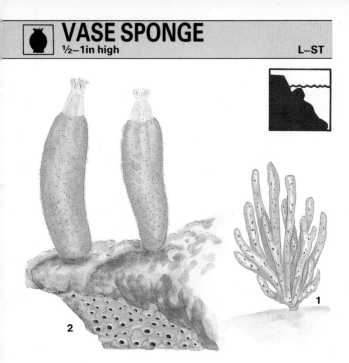

Vase- or bottle-shaped. Cream to tan in color and fuzzy in texture. A single opening at the top is surrounded by a fringe of glassy spicules. Immobile, it grows attached to hard substrates in clusters of up to 10 individuals.

Sponges are the simplest multi-celled animals and lack body organs. Water is drawn into central body cavity by small pores and expelled through one larger opening. Oxygen and food particles taken up by body cells are exchanged for waste matter.

Attached to rocks, pilings, harbor floats and seaweeds. Lower shore and below. East coast from Arctic to Rhode Island, West coast from British Columbia to Central California.

Finger Sponge (**1:**) 18in. Subtidal. Lab.–N.C. **Breadcrumb Sponge** (**2:**) 12in. wide. Yellow. Encrusting under rocks. Arc.–C.Cod; Alas.–S.Cal. Red species **toxic** (blisters.) Fla., Gulf, W.I.

Highly variable: deep red to chestnut or purplish, may be streaked or blotched with greenish brown. Smooth column often with shell and gravel fragments stuck to it. 80–160 short retractile tentacles, often ringed with pale and darker color bands. Strongly adhesive sucker-like base.

Several color varieties have been identified (see below,) although thought by some to be separate species. When exposed at low tide, anemone contracts and completely encloses the tentacles.

On rocks, in crevices, under rocky overhangs or seaweeds, shaded from bright light. In sheltered pools; mid to low tide. Arctic to Casco Bay, Maine, rare to Cape Cod; Alaska to central California.

Strawberry Anemone (1:) scarlet; few tubercles; tentacles unbanded; Wash.–C.Cal. **Leathery Anemone (2:)** brownish; many adhesive tubercles; banded tentacles; Alas.–C.Cal.

31

Pale brown, olive, orange, pink, cream or white. Column smooth, well-developed collar visible below crown of feathery tentacles. Ejects long white threads of stinging cells when disturbed. Basal disk adhesive.

Can reproduce asexually by dividing body in half or leaving small portions of the basal disk which regenerate into new individuals. Juveniles do not always resemble adults and may be difficult to identify.

Common on lower shore and waters down to 500ft. On rocks, in crevices and pools, wharves, docks and pilings. Arctic to Delaware Bay; Alaska to Southern California.

Found with other common anemones, but has many more, finer tentacles. **Ghost Anemone** is similar to juveniles but lacks threads of stinging cells.

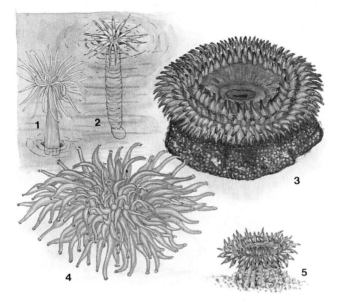

Ghost Anemone (**1**) 1½in. tall. White, pinkish to olive. Slender, smooth column with tiny dark bumps. 40–60 long tentacles around mouth. Common under rocks, on pilings, stones & shells. Me.–N.C.; Cal.

Elegant Burrowing Anemone (**2**) 1½in. Worm-like, red-yellowish. Warty grooved column & lower digging organ. Burrows in muddy sand & gravel, 16 red-striped tentacles extended over surface. Low tide & below. N.B.–Ches. Bay. Other species Cal.

Giant Green Anemone (**3**) 7in. wide. Tentacles emerald green, bluish or white. Sand & shell fragments on warty olive green column. Rocks & pilings, pools, exposed coasts. Low tide & below. Not in polluted water. Alas.–Pan.

Pink-tipped Anemone (**4**) Up to 12in. wide. White, bluish, pink, orange, or reddish. Tentacles tipped pink, scarlet, blue or green. On rocks in shallow water around reefs. S. Fla.–W.I.

Aggregating Anemone (**5**) 2in. wide. Column olive green, white, pink or blue, adhesive tubercles covered with sand & shell pieces. Divides to form dense groups. Rocks & pilings. Intertidal. Alas.–Mex.

33

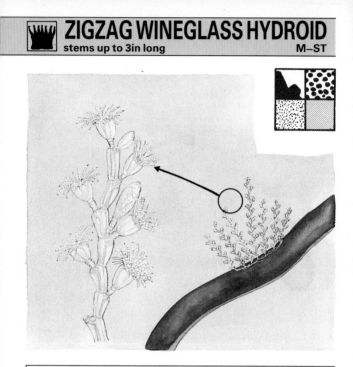

Whitish colony of tiny anemone-like creatures (polyps.) Erect, zigzag branching stems joined by creeping roots. Polyps in wineglass-shaped cups are borne on alternate sides of the stem. Reproductive buds are vase-shaped.

Individual polyps are joined to others by tubes running throughout the colony branches. Reproductive buds release tiny medusa (jellyfish) to float in plankton. Colony often only comprises a few stalks, but may form extensive mats 12in. wide.

Mid-shore to shallow water on rock weeds, kelps, Sargasso weed, rocks and pilings. Widespread from British Columbia to Southern California, Arctic to Florida, and Texas. West Indies.

There are many similar hydroids, difficult to distinguish. Garland Hydroids form bushy colonies up to 12in. long. No medusa stage. East and west coasts.

1

2

Bushy, tufted colony of microscopic animals (zooids,) easily mistaken for seaweed. Double rows of zooids wind spirally around branches. Yellow to orange brown, fading to white. Colonies occasionally grow to 12 inches.

The minute zooids live in individual box- or vase-like exoskeletons, variously joined together to form the colony. Passing food particles are trapped by a ring of tentacles surrounding the zooid's mouth.

Lower shore to shallow waters (90ft.) on many substrates, eelgrass, seaweeds, rocks, stones, pilings, shells. Often washed ashore and in estuaries. Bay of Fundy to Florida. California Spiral-tufted Bryozoan occurs on west coast.

Sea Lichen Bryozoan (1:) 1½in. Yellowish flattened branches. Low tide. E. and W. species similar. **Lacy Crust (2:)** 3in. wide. Encrusting on kelps, other substrates. Low to subtidal. E.,W.

35

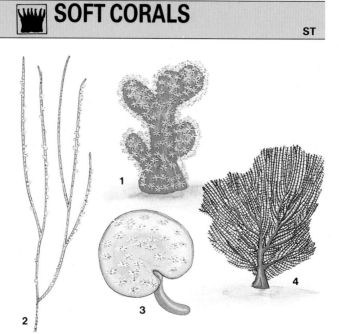

Red Soft Coral (**1**) 6in. high. Soft & fleshy with finger-like branches growing from a central stalk. Red-orange with white polyps each with 8 short tentacles. Below low tide level, on rocks, pilings, rocky pools. Arc.–Me.; Alas.–N. Cal. Dead Man's Fingers similar but pinkish to pale orange. G. St. Law.–R.I.

Sea Whip (**2**) To 3ft. long. Stem & branches whip-like with tough pitted skin & horny core. Purple, red, orange-yellow, tan. Low tide & below on rocks, jetties, pilings. C. Hatt. to G. Mex. Unbranched. Straight Sea Whip found N. to Patuxent River, Md.

Sea Pansy (**3**) 2in. long. Flat like thick, fleshy lilypad. Polyps on upper surface. White to yellowish, or pink to purple. Muscular purple stalk. Bioluminescent. In shallow water with stalk buried in sand. C. Hat.–Fla. & W.I. Similar species in G. Mex. & S. Cal.

Sea Fan (**4**) 3ft. tall. Oval in outline but very flattened, formed of many net-like branches fused into latticework. Pink-purple to deep red or yellowish. Shallow waters, on rocks around coral reef. S. Fla., Ber. & W.I. Often dried for sale as souvenirs.

Colony bush-like with many cylindrical branches, 1in. wide, not fused together. Branches yellow to purplish brown with pale tips. Polyps in small raised cups orientated toward the tip of each branch.

Stony coral polyps are similar to sea anemones, but sit in chalky cups which they have secreted around their base and sides, forming a cup. Polyps reproduce to form a colony which secretes a complex skeleton.

On windward side of coral reefs in waters of 10 feet or more. Florida Keys, Bahamas and West Indies. Coral reefs only develop in clear waters in sheltered warm seas (optimum temperature 23–25°C.)

Related Elkhorn Coral (5ft. wide) has flattened fan-like branches. Cream to brownish yellow, with white tips. Cups orientated toward growing edge. **CUTS** on contact, slow to heal.

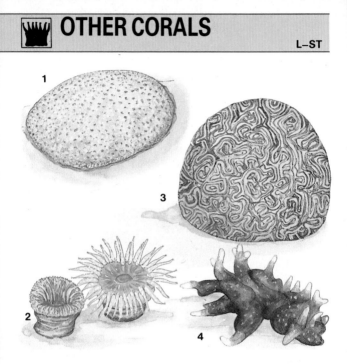

Starlet Coral (**1**) 12in. wide. Common on shallow reef flats. Encrusting when young, grows to a rounded mass. Pink, brown, yellow or gray. Star-like cups, ⅛in. Tolerate variation in temperature & salinity. Fla. & G. Mex.–Mex., Ber., Bah.; W.I.–S. America.

Orange Cup Coral (**2**) ⅜in. Solitary orange-yellow anemone-like polyp in single stony cup with radial internal divisions (septae.) In shade under rocks on exposed coasts & in bays. Low tide–70ft. Only intertidal stony coral from B. Col.–Baja Cal.

Labyrinthine Brain Coral (**3**) Forms massive rounded boulders to 8ft. in diameter. Polyps in deeply folded rows with valleys between (¼in. deep, ⅜in. wide.) Resembles human brain. Shallow water & on reefs. Fla. & Gulf coast–Mex., Ber., Bah., W.I.

Fire Coral (**4**) 24in. high, 18in. wide. Branching or plate-like, brown, cream or yellowish; white branch tips. White polyps in pores over surface. On coral reefs or encrusting shells, horny corals, pilings, etc. **TOXIC**: severe burns & blistering rash. Fla.–Mex., Bah., W.I.

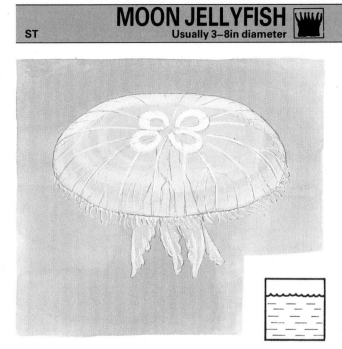

Saucer-shaped umbrella may reach 16in. diameter. Translucent white to bluish with many short tentacles. Under umbrella, mouth is surrounded by 4 longer purplish arms with frilly margins. 4 conspicuous white, yellow or purple reproductive organs around center appear horseshoe-shaped from above.

Swim by opening and closing umbrella in a continuous pulsating action. **Mildly toxic:** a sting results in a rash that may itch for several hours. Stinging cells are located in arms and tentacles. Feed on small animals floating in the plankton.

Common in surface waters just offshore. Atlantic coasts from Arctic to Florida and Mexico, Pacific coasts from Alaska to Baja California. Large numbers occur where sea temperatures are higher than normal: docks, harbors, power station outfalls.

White-cross Jellyfish has a conspicuous white cross on the umbrella and longer tentacles; it occurs along east coast from Arctic to Rhode Island.

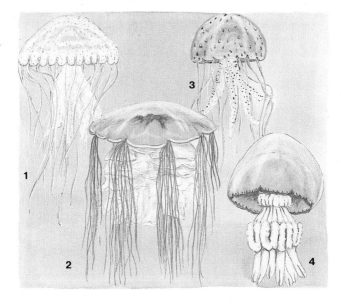

Sea Nettle (1) Umbrella 8in. dia., pinkish, pimpled, 40 marginal tentacles. Feeding tube beneath umbrella, 4 long frilly lips. **TOXIC**: sharp sting itches. C. Cod–Tex. Common Ches. Bay. Lined Sea Nettle: similar; Alas.– S. Cal.

Lion's Mane (2) Umbrella 5– 18in. dia., rarely 3–8ft. Pink to yellow-brown. Shaggy tentacles hang from 8 clusters beneath. Feeding tube has 4 frilly lips, alternate with ribbon-like gonads. **HIGHLY TOXIC**: severe burns, possibly muscle cramps & breathing difficulties. Arc.–Fla. & Mex.; Alas.–S. Cal.

Purple Jellyfish (3) Warty umbrella 4in. dia. Pink, purple or yellow. 8 pink marginal tentacles & warty sense organs. Feeding tube; 4 long, frilly lips. Luminescent. Large swarms off E. & W. coasts. **HIGHLY TOXIC**. Purple Banded Jellyfish: 32in., with purple radiating bands; W.

Cannonball Jellyfish (4) Umbrella 7in. dia. White to blue or yellowish. Tough. 128 small marginal lobes often purple. No tentacles. Stout arms surround feeding tube. In swarms, cast up in large numbers. Tex.–Fla., N. to Ches. Bay; Bah. & W.I.

1

Gas-filled float, tapering at one end, has deflatable sail-like crest. Silvery blue tinged with pink and purple. Blue-purple tentacles of varying lengths suspended beneath. **HIGHLY TOXIC:** do not touch tentacles with bare hands, cause severe burns even when dead. Float often detached in beached specimens.

Float conspicuous on surface of water, but beware when swimming as tentacles may trail for some 50 feet behind. Tentacles are a complex colony of 3 types of zooids, specialized for fishing and defense (stinging cells,) feeding, and reproduction.

Lives on open ocean. Gulf Stream, Florida to Texas and Mexico, Bahamas and West Indies. Cast ashore by storms on the east coast, as far north as Cape Cod and, rarely, into the Gulf of Maine.

By-the-wind Sailor (**1**:) 4in. Oval float with triangular sail. Glassy bluish or amber. Harmless blue tentacles beneath. Warm seas, cast ashore. Gulf Stream, N. to C. Hatt.; C. Cal. to Mex.

41

Slender, vase-like body contracts readily. Translucent, yellowish to pale green. 5 longitudinal muscle bands and digestive system visible through body wall. 2 openings (siphons) near top ringed with yellow and red spots. Water squirts from siphons when body is gently squeezed.

These sea squirts are filter feeders and have a pharynx with gill slits for respiration and feeding. Simple in form, but closely related to higher vertebrate animals. A fouling species, they are transported worldwide on ships' hulls.

On rocks, harbor structures, pilings, floats and hulls. Lower shore to waters 1650ft. deep. Pacific coast from Alaska to Southern California. Arctic to Rhode Island in the east.

Vase Sponge: immobile. **Golden Star Tunicate (1:)** encrusting 4in. wide. Individuals form stars round common opening. B. Fundy to N.C. Other species North to South California.

Irregular cucumber-shaped animal. Dark purplish brown, paler beneath. 5 bands of orange tube feet run along sides of body, 2 above, 3 on lower surface. 10 highly branched tentacles surround mouth, often the only part visible.

Related to Sea Urchins and Sea Stars, soft-bodied with a few calcareous "deposits" embedded in skin. Filter feeders, collecting plankton and detritus with tentacles. If roughly handled, may eject internal organs, later regenerated.

Rocky shores, pools, often in crevices with only tentacles visible at the surface. Low tide level to waters 1200ft. deep (deep water specimens reach 19in. in length.) Arctic to Cape Cod. Other southern species.

Red Sea Cucumber: 10in. Brick red, orange or purple. In crevices and under rocks. Low tide to shallow waters. In algal holdfasts in Monterey Bay; Alaska to Central California.

43

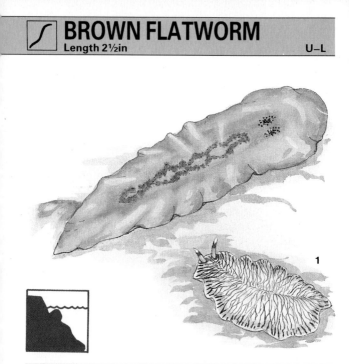

Leaf-like body is flat and unsegmented, tapering to a pointed tail. Tan to pale gray with brown patches along mid-line. The head bears paired clusters of eyespots and the mouth is located centrally, beneath the lower surface. Margins wavy.

These are simple animals with no body cavity, a sac-like gut, but no anus. They are very active, gliding over rocks in search of food like limpets, barnacles and other small animals. Some flatworms swim by undulating their body margins.

Found mostly on rocky shores. Extremely common under rocks from high to low tide zones on the California coast and elsewhere in the west.

Speckled Flatworm: a similar species found in New England. **Crozier's Flatworm** (1) is brightly patterned with paired tentacles; common at low tide and shallow water, Fla. and W.I.

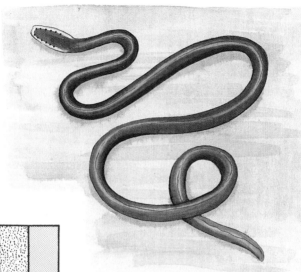

Very long worm with unsegmented, slightly flattened body. Color is variable from red-brown to greenish, paler below. 4–8 eyespots and a sensory groove occur on each side of the head. The body narrows behind the head.

Long elastic body contracts by shortening and thickening; some other species form tight coils. A long proboscis is extruded to catch prey, usually small worms and crustaceans.

Found beneath stones and shells, amongst algae and mussels on sandy and muddy beaches. From mid-shore level down to shallow water. Tolerates brackish water. Maine to Long Island in the east, Washington to central California in the west.

Many species are highly colored, some spotted or striped. Wandering Nemertean is 10in. long and often seen crawling on surface of mudflats. Common from Alaska to Mexico.

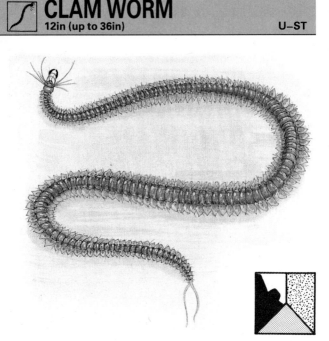

Large, active worm with many body segments bearing paddle-like parapodia and bristles. Bluish green, iridescent purple on back, parapodia bordered with yellow. Pale, pinkish below. Head bears tentacles, acorn-like palps and 4 eyes. Eversible proboscis bears teeth and a pair of large black jaws.

Voracious predator feeding on small invertebrates, carrion and algae. Prey is taken by rapidly unrolling proboscis to expose and open jaws. Rolling back closes jaws and draws food into mouth. Can inflict a painful **bite**. Excellent fishing bait.

Upper shore to shallow waters 500 feet deep. Rocky, sandy and muddy shores, amongst surf grass roots, algae and boulders. Often burrows into sand. Sheltered waters and estuaries on Pacific coast and from Maine to Virginia in the east.

Several smaller clam worms are common on east, west and south coasts. Pelagic Clam Worm is 6in. long, red-brown to olive, with short tentacles. Low shore and shallow water, E. and W.

Long, slender worms with body segments extended into large leaf-like paddles which fold over the back. Whitish, brown, green, gray or purplish, often darker along the back. Head bears tentacles and two prominent eyes. Eversible proboscis is not armed with jaws.

Preying on other small worms and invertebrates, and preyed upon by fish. As they crawl, the leafy paddles move in a wave-like sequence which passes down the body.

Amongst mussels and barnacles, in sand and mud under rocks, amongst shells and gravel. Often in algal holdfasts. Lower shore down to 5000ft.

Green Paddle Worm is 6in. long and grass-green; cosmopolitan, Arc. to N.J. California Black-striped Paddle Worm similar with stripes between segments; common in N. Cal.

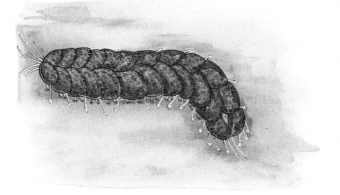

A small segmented worm. Upper surface of body covered by 12 pairs of oval, overlapping scales. Color is mottled brown, gray, tan or yellowish. Head and tail bear long tentacles. Shorter tentacles and bristles grow from the sides of each body segment.

Rolls into a ball when disturbed. Less likely to lose scales than some species which readily detach their scales when handled. For this reason, try to count the scales on these worms before disturbing them.

Cosmopolitan. Mid-shore down to waters at least 8000ft. deep. Free-living in rocky habitats, under boulders, amongst algae, gravel and shell bottoms, pilings. From Labrador to New Jersey in the east, Alaska to California in the west.

Commensal 12-scaled Worm: lives with hermit crabs; E. 15-scaled Worm: E., W. 18-scaled Worm: E., W. Pacific Scale Worm: 30 pairs scales; W. Burrowing Scale Worm: 150 pairs; E., W.

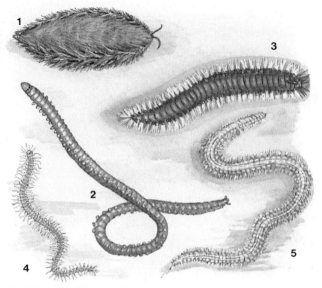

Sea Mouse (**1**) 6in. long, 3in. wide. Scales masked by mat of brownish, often iridescent scales covering back. Subtidal on sand & mud. Dredged or washed ashore after storms. G. St. Law.–N.J. Similar species in Cal.

Opal Worm (**2**) 24in. long. Slender, red-brown, yellow or greenish iridescent. Head conical, no tentacles. Sand & sandy mud, mussel & eelgrass beds, estuaries. W. coast & Mass. to Fla. & Tex.

Orange Fire Worm (**3**) 6in. Orange-yellow with frilly red gills & tufts of white bristles on sides. Bristles are **HIGHLY TOXIC**: painful sting.

Under rocks, low tide & below. E: Fla., C. Mex., W.I. W: S. Cal.

Syllis gracilis (Syllid Worm) (**4**) 2in. long. Common in bottom debris, algae and rock crevices. Gray to reddish yellow. Long, jointed tentacles on head & each body segment. E: C. Cod–Me. W: Cal.

Shimmy Worm (**5**) 8–12in. long. Similar to clam worms, but head squarish with stumpy antennae. Pearly gray with red blood vessels visible down back & belly. Common, active predator in sand or mud. Lower shore, E. & W. Several similar species hard to distinguish.

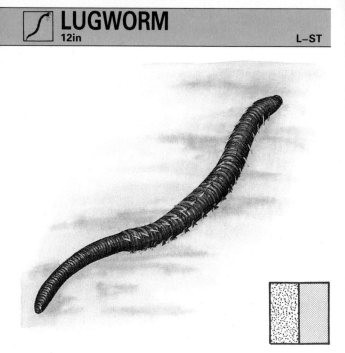

Robust, burrowing worm. Greenish black cylindrical body with last third forming narrower tail. Ringed body segments carry paired tufts of bristles and 11 pairs of red feathery gills on the middle third of the body. Tapered head lacks appendages and eyes. Tail has no bristles or gills.

Lugworms make U-shaped burrows: collapsed front end marked by a depression in sand, rear by a small formless heap. Eat sand from below front of tube, with food particles filtered from irrigation currents. Undigested sand deposited at tube exit.

In sand and muddy sand, in sheltered bays and creeks. Lower shore. Pacific coast and from Cape Cod to Florida and Louisiana in the east.

Northern Lugworm: 8in. 12–13 pairs of gills. Arctic to Cape Cod. Forms rope-like casts of sand. Good fishing bait.

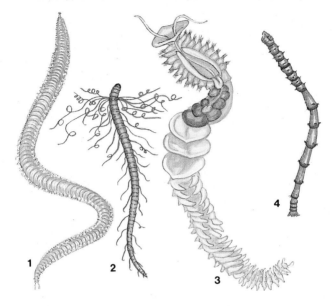

Blood Worm (1) Up to 15in. long. Retractable gills. Rapidly everts large bulbous proboscis bearing 4 teeth. **Bites.** Sold for bait. Sand & mud flats. Low tide to 1300ft. Several similar species, E., W. & Gulf coasts.

Eyed Fringed Worm (2) 4in. Orange cylindrical worm. Indistinct head has 2–9 pairs of eyes. 4th or 5th segment bears cluster of red filaments, often in tightly coiled mass, easily broken. Red gills on rest of body. In mud tubes under rocks etc. Lower shore. Pacific coast; Me.–Cape Cod. Similar species N. Eng.–Gulf of Mexico.

Parchment Worm (3) 10in. Flabby, fragile, luminescent yellow-green body in 3 distinct parts. Head has large mouth & 2 tentacles. 3 flap-like paddles in mid-body pump water. In large U-shaped tube lined with leathery, white membrane, projects above mud surface. Low tide & shallow waters in sheltered mud & sand. C. Cod–Fla.; La., C. & S. Cal.

Bamboo Worm (4) 6in. long, thin with few, bamboo-like segments. Red or green color deeper at joints. In vertical tube in sand or mud, low tide to 300ft. Me.–N.C. Similar species in Cal.

51

ICE CREAM CONE WORM
1⅝in; tube 2½in   L–ST

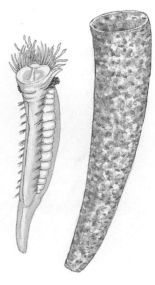

This worm builds a slightly curved, cone-shaped tube of sand grains. The flattened head has 2 pairs of antennae and paired combs of 15 iridescent golden bristles.

Tube is constructed from a single layer of sand grains, selected for type and size, and cemented with mucus. Worms lie buried head down, with only open point of cone exposed above sand. Empty tubes may often be found on beaches.

Sand and muddy sand on open coastlines and estuaries. Lower shore to shallow waters. Bay of Fundy to Florida.

Californian Ice Cream Cone Worm: straight tube of fine red-brown sand. Coarse-grained Ice Cream Cone Worm: curved tube of coarse black and white grains. Both Alaska to Baja Cal.

1

Stout worm in a tough leathery tube sticking out of the ground. Body divided into short thorax and longer abdomen, cream, pink to orange in color. Mouth surrounded by branchial crown of 24 feathery filaments, patterned with red bands. 2–6 pairs of eyespots on midrib of each branchial filament.

Branchial crown, only extended underwater, acts as both gills and filter feeding organ. At low tide, withdraws deep into tube, so best observed in tide pools and shallow water. Reacts instantly to shadows by withdrawing into tube.

Attached to rocks and shells, pilings, in mixed mud, sand and gravel. Lower shore to waters 170ft. deep. Pacific coast and Maine to Cape Cod.

Slime Fan Worm (**1**:) 8 in. Thick jelly-like tube. Funnel-shaped branchial crown on surface of sand or mud. Pacific; Me. to N.Y. Giant Fan Worm: 10in. Various colors. Pacific tidepools.

Plump, soft-bodied molluscs with a small, internal shell. Head bears a pair of antennae which resemble hare's ears. Smaller antennae located over mouth. 2 wing-like flaps along back. Brown, patterned with black net-like pattern and silvery specks.

Browse seaweeds and kelp or swim slowly by beating their wings. Body color changes from red to brown to olive green with age and weeds eaten. Long, sticky, pinkish egg strings laid around seaweeds. May release harmless purple dye when handled.

Low tide and below in sheltered shallow waters, amongst seaweeds and eelgrass beds. Gulf of Mexico to North Carolina. May also, but rarely, occur further north, as far as Cape Cod.

Spotted Sea Hare: 5in. Yellow-olive with dark circles. Florida, Texas, West Indies. California Black Sea Hare: to 30in. long, one of largest gastropods. Reddish black. S. to Baja Cal.

Soft body is covered, except in mid-line, by numerous finger-like cerata. Color whitish pink, gray or brown. Head blunt, two pairs of tentacles, tapering tail. Other species have fewer cerata.

Feed on sea anemones and adopt their color. Have no shells but deter predators with foul taste and stinging cells incorporated into cerata from prey. Spiral ribbons or grape-like clusters of eggs. Observe alive, they die out of water.

Common on rocky shores, between tidemarks and in shallow water. Usually with anemones, on wharves, in tidal pools, often on undersurface of boulders. Alaska to S. California; Arctic to Cape Cod and, rarely, south to Ocean City, Maryland.

Hermissenda (1:) 3¼in. Dorsal yellow stripe. Common. W.
Rough-mantled Doris (2:) 1in. Brown-cream. Oval. Rear gill ring. B. Fundy to R.I.; Alas. to Baja Cal.

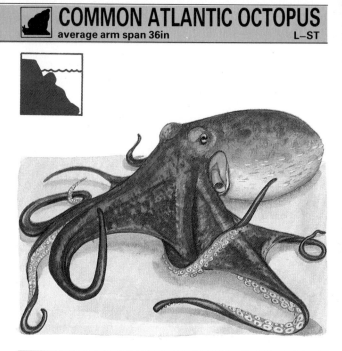

Bulbous body with 4 pairs of arms, each bearing 2 rows of suckers. 2 prominent eyes and a siphon tube located at neck level. Skin smooth or warty. Color variable depending on habitat, reddish brown, gray to green.

Secretive: hides in crevices among rocks, may arrange stones for camouflage and protection. Uses arms to crawl over bottom but swims by jet propulsion when alarmed. Mouth with beak-like jaws located beneath base of arms.

Among rocks and stones, coral reefs. Low tide level to deep waters (some deep water specimens have 10ft. arm span.) Common from Southern Florida to Texas and Mexico; West Indies. Rare further north.

Two-spotted Octopus: 30in. arm span. 2 blue-ringed eyespots. Low tide to 160ft. C.Cal to Gulf of Cal. Giant Pacific Octopus: intertidal, Alas. to Ore.; reddish with black lines.

Elongate, cylindrical body, tapered toward rear, with long, paired, triangular fins. Head has 2 large eyes. 4 pairs of arms and one longer pair of tentacles bear small suckers. Siphon under neck. Color white, mottled red, brown, purple or yellow. Body soft and flabby out of water.

Fast swimmers in large schools, prey on fish, crustaceans and other squid. Eaten by bluefish, sea bass, mackerel and caught commercially for bait and markets. Release cloud of ink when threatened. Can change body color instantly.

Ocean surface waters to 300ft. deep. Abundant in shallow waters during summer. Bay of Fundy to West Indies. Common from Cape Hatteras to Cape Cod.

Opalescent Squid (Calamari:) 7in. Abundant offshore from B.C. to Mex. Fished commercially in C. and S. Cal. Cylindrical white gelatinous egg masses may be washed ashore.

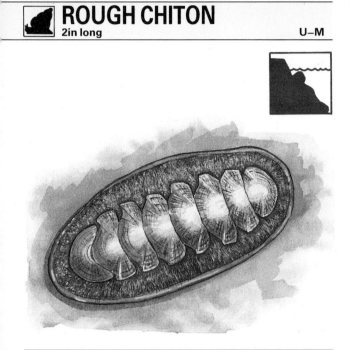

Oval, covered with 8 calcareous plates surrounded by a fleshy girdle. Muscular foot forms lower surface, with gills on either side, head and mouth at front. Brown girdle mossy, with short brown rigid spines and orange underside. Plates brown to grayish streaked white, often eroded along central ridge.

Firmly stuck to rocks by broad foot, less mobile than other chitons. May return "home" to same depression in rock. When dislodged, partially rolls up to protect soft underparts. Uses scraping mouthparts to graze red and green algae.

One of the commonest intertidal chitons found on the west coast. High to mid-tide level on rocks exposed to surf, crevices, or on barnacle and mussel beds. Puget Sound to Mexico.

See **Other Chitons**.

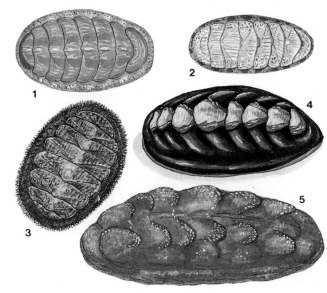

Red Chiton (**1**) Plates reddish, smooth with central ridge. Girdle granular, red & white bands. Lower shore, common on & under rocks. Arc.–Mass. Bay. Subtidal to L.I. Sound.

Bee Chiton (**2**) ¾in. Plates cream, gray-brown. Central area with pattern of fine lines. Girdle mottled brown-cream, granular, scattered short hairs. 24 pairs gills. Common. Low tide. C. Cod–W. Fla.

Mossy Chiton (**3**) 2–3½in. Broad, flattened, dark olive, brown-gray. Girdle with dense mossy hairs. Fine ridges on plates. On protected rocks, tidal pools, high-low tide. Alas.–Cal.

Black Chiton (**4**) 2¾–4¾in. Smooth black girdle covers most of white plates. Foot red-salmon color. With **Rough Chiton** on exposed rocks, with **coralline algae** & **mussels**, mid-low tide. Alas.–Point Conception. Tolerates waves & sunlight.

Gumboot (**5**) 6–13in. World's largest chiton. Girdle brick red, gritty, completely covers plates. Isolated white plates (butterfly shells) cast onto beaches. Among rocks, mid-low tide. Alas.–Channel Is., Cal., but scarce Monterey & south.

1

Thick, low, cone-shaped shell with apex just off center. Color variable, green or brownish gray with irregular paler spotting, rarely solid color. Large muscular foot beneath holds limpet firmly to the substrate. Head bears a pair of tentacles and mouth with rasping tongue.

As tide rises, crawl over rocks grazing algal films; when tide falls, return to resting spot, often same slight depression in rock. To avoid predators and dislodging by surf, limpets clamp tight to rock face, their shell acting as a suction cup.

Rocky shores, high to low tide on rocks exposed to moderate surf. Alaska to southern California.

Tortoiseshell Limpet (Atlantic Plate Limpet) (**1:**) ⅞–1¾in. Similar but now considered distinct from Pacific species. Radiating red-brown bands, often checkered. Arc. to L.I. Sound.

Owl Limpet (1) To 4in. Low shell with apex near front. Light brown with irregular, radial white spots. Pushes intruders off home territory. Undersides of rocks, in strong surf, high-mid tide. Cape Flattery–Mex. Largest N. American limpet, sold as souvenirs.

Rough Limpet (2) 1¼in. Radiating light-colored ribs & scalloped margin. Grayish with irregular darker pattern. Shell apex off center. Black spots on head & sides of foot. High tide, on horizontal rocks with barnacles. Homing behavior. Abundant. Ore.–Mex.

Keyhole Limpet (3) 1–2½in. Conical. Hole at apex vents waste water. Gray-brown to whitish, radiating dark ribs crossed by concentric lines. Under rocks, low tide. Alas.–Mex.

Black Abalone (4) 6in. Oval, flattened shell, greenish black to dark blue, small apex at rear, row of 6–8 holes across upper surface, pearly inside. In deep crevices washed by strong waves & currents, high-low tide & shallow water. Ore.–Mex. Blood does not coagulate: bleed to death if cut. Edible but overcollected.

Arched, boat-shaped shell. Small apex at rear turned to one side. Tan colored, speckled brown and purple. A white shelf-like platform, extending halfway across opening of shell, has a sinuous edge. Large muscular foot, head and tentacles buff.

Permanently attached by the foot to any hard object, these animals form a stack of individuals which undergo a sex-change during life. Small shells are male, but as they grow larger and others settle upon them, they become female.

Lower shore, often on sand or muddy gravel. Pest of oyster beds (smother shells.) Empty shells may be abundant, cast onto protected beaches. Gulf of St. Lawrence to Florida and Texas. Introduced with oysters to Central California.

Convex Slipper Shell: ½in.; concave-edged platform over ⅓rd of opening; interior brown. Low tide, Mass. Bay to Gulf of Mexico; locally N. to G. St. Law.; introduced to San Francisco Bay.

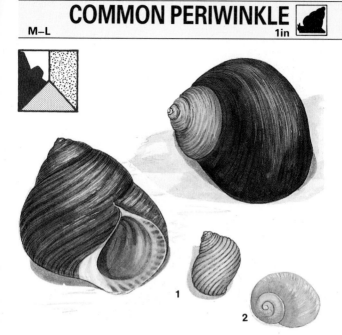

Solid, conical snail with blunt spire and rounded aperture. Dark gray to black, often with concentric darker lines but no ridges in adult; inner lip white. Head, tentacles and foot gray, mottled. Retreats into shell and seals aperture with horny operculum.

Browse on algal films, following a circular route as tide goes out, returning to "home" area as tide returns. Also migrate up and down beach in breeding season. Tolerate lack of food and dry conditions. Edible, eaten in Europe.

Rocky shores, on rocks and algae. Also on muddy sands. Mid to low tide. Common Maryland to Labrador. Locally introduced to C. California. Eroded Periwinkle: ¾in.; pointed spire, eroded tip; brown and white; rocks at high tide, Oregon to Mexico.

Rough Periwinkle (**1**:) ½in. Pointed spire, ridged, yellowish to red-brown. On rocks, high tide. Arc. to N.J. **Smooth Periwinkle** (**2**:) ½in. Flat spire. On rockweed, low tide. Lab. to N.J.

Stout, thick conical or dome-shaped, apex often eroded. Purple-black to black, pearly white below and inside. Scaly band or cords below suture. Aperture round, sealed by operculum. Older specimens have 2 teeth on columella. Head and foot black.

A top shell, one of the most abundant snails on west coast beaches. Form large congregations in crevices at low tide. Feed on fleshy algae. Individuals may live for 25 years. Empty shells used by hermit crabs.

Rocky shores, but avoids exposed outer coast and extensive weed cover. Mid-tide. British Columbia (Vancouver) to central Baja California.

Brown Turban: 1¾in.; no scaly band, 1 tooth on columella when older; brown; foot has orange border. Lower shore and offshore kelp beds near surface. Cape Arago, Ore. to Santa Barbara Is.

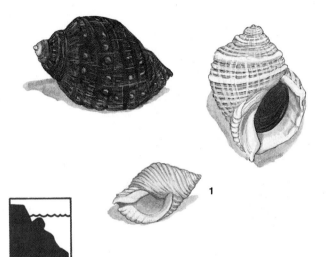

1

Thick, rounded whelk-shaped shell with large body whorl. Highly variable: yellow, brown, white, gray or black, smooth or with spiral, often knobby, cords and thin spiral ribs between. Often banded. Curved columella, short siphonal canal, large oval aperture with flaring lip and horny brown operculum.

Usually found near mussel beds, eating young mussels and barnacles by boring through shells. Prefer Blue to Californian mussels. Types of food may affect shell coloration. Eggs laid in clusters of flask-like horny capsules.

Rocky shores, on rocks and in crevices. Common to abundant in high tide zone. Alaska to Mexico, but less common south of Point Conception.

Atlantic Dogwinkle (1:) 1½in. Variable, whitish, yellow to brown, banded, smooth or ridged. Aperture has thick lip. Similar diet. Grain-like egg capsules. L.I. Sound–Arctic.

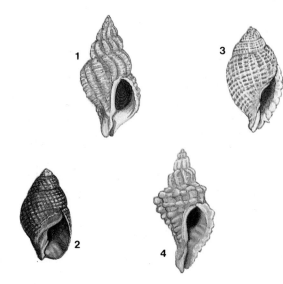

Spotted Unicorn (3) 1½in.
Smooth, brownish with white
lines & rows of dark rectangles
between. Aperture brownish
white inside, outer lip with
projections & 1 short spine when
older. Short siphonal canal.
Upper shore on rocks or in tide
pools at low tide. Monterey,
Cal.–Mex.

Atlantic Oyster Drill (1) ½–
1¾in. Gray to yellowish white,
strong axial ribs. Often banded.
Open siphonal canal, aperture
lip thickened. Major pest of
oyster beds: bores hole in shell
with radula. Intertidal to 50ft.
Fla.–G. St. Law.; Wash.–C.
Cal.

Mud Dog Whelk (2) ⅝–1¼in.
Thick, reddish brown, apex
eroded. Slanting axial ribs & low
spiral cords. Aperture brown-
black, glazed inside. On
intertidal mud & below. G.
Mex.–G. St. Law.; Vancouver
Is.–C. Cal.

Carpenter's Dwarf Triton (4)
⅞in. Gray to yellowish, whorls
have flattened shoulder & heavy
lattice-like sculpture. Oval
aperture, flared lip. Siphonal
canal open or closed. Common
under algae-covered rocks.
Inter-tidal & below Alas.–N.
Baja Cal.

LARGE WHELKS

Common Northwest Neptune
(1) 5in. Heavy, whitish, spindle-shaped shell, conical spire & backward curved open siphonal canal. Rounded body whorls with 7–10 reddish brown spiral cords. White columella twisted, aperture white or tan; oval, horny operculum. Head & foot pale gray, dark speckled. Atlantic Ten-ridged Whelk is probably same species. Sand or mud, low tide to 300ft. Arc.–C. Cal.; N.S.–C. Cod. Channeled Whelk, 7in., has long siphon. In Mud. C. Cod–N. Fla. & G. Mex.

Waved Whelk (2) 3in. Body whorl with axial ribs & spiral cords, whitish to tan. Subtidal, ploughs through sediments. Shells & round spongy egg capsules washed ashore. Edible. Arc.–N.J. Offshore S. of C. Cod.

Scotch Bonnet (3) 4in. Whitish with orange-brown square spots, many spiral grooves. Large aperture has heavy toothed outer lip. Subtidal, shells on N.C. beaches inhabited by Striped Hermit Crab. Feeds on Sand Dollars & urchins. N.C.–Fla. & Tex., W.I.–Brazil.

67

Florida Fighting Conch (1) 3–
4in. Heavy knobby shell, cream
to chestnut. Large body whorl.
Subtidal on sand. N.C.–Mex.
Banded Tulip (2) 3in. Mottled
white, brown spiral lines. Sand
& mud, low-subtidal. N.C.–
Tex., Bah. & W.I.
Lace Murex (3) 3in. Spiny,
white to brown. Subtidal on
mud, sand & coral rubble.
N.C.–G. Mex.; Bah., W.I.
Alphabet Cone (4) 3in. Cone-
shaped, white with orange-
brown squares. Subtidal.
TOXIC: bee-like sting. Fla., G.
Mex., W.I.

Beautiful shells, glossy & colorful as fleshy mantle covers most of shell in life. Often at risk from overcollection.

Coffee Bean Trivia (**1**) ½–¾in. Pinkish to coffee colored, with white ribs. 3 pairs of dark brown spots on back. Long narrow aperture. With compound ascidians (its prey.) Lower shore & shallow water. N.C.–Brazil.

Purple Dwarf Olive (**2**) 1¼in. Whitish to brown, violet tints. Dark suture line, short apex. Long aperture. Foot & mantle cream, long siphon tube. Common in clean sand of sloping protected beaches. Offshore in exposed locations. B.C.–Baja Cal.

Deer Cowrie (**3**) 3–5in. Oval, long slit-like toothed aperture below. Brownish with white spots above, paler below. Head bears 2 tentacles, short siphon tube above. N.C.–Fla., Ber. & Cuba.

Flamingo Tongue (**4**) 1¾in. Blunt spindle-shaped, ridge across back, long & slit-like aperture. Cream to apricot, unpatterned but yellow, black-rimmed spots on fleshy mantle may stick to shell. Subtidal, on sea fans & other soft corals: feeds on these at night. N.C.–Fla., W.I.

Large heavy shell with rounded body whorl, shallow groove between flattened shoulder and suture. Yellowish white to pale brown. Deep umbilicus covered by brown columnar callus. Large horny operculum closes oval to semicircular aperture.

A very large foot partly shields shell as the animal ploughs through sand and mud searching for small clams. A small hole drilled through the clam enables its soft parts to be eaten. Eggs are embedded in characteristic "sand collars."

Common on sand and mudflats in bays, lagoons and eelgrass beds. Shallow waters to 600ft deep. Vancouver Island, British Columbia to northern Baja California.

Shark Eye: 3in.; umbilical callus, no suture groove. Gray-tan. Mass. Bay–G. Mex., rarer N. to B. Fundy. Northern Moon Shell: 4½in.; no callus. Lab.–N.C. Both sand, mud; low tide to 1200ft.

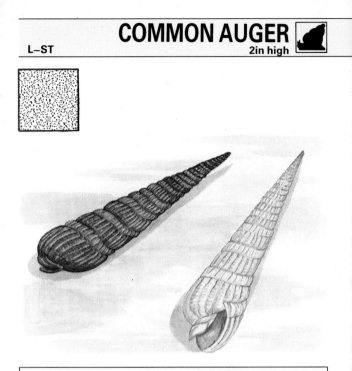

A tall cone, tapering to a sharp point. Pinkish gray, bluish or yellowish. 25 ribs to each whorl, with fine spiral lines and beaded band beneath suture. Small aperture and siphonal canal twisted at base of columella.

Augers burrow into sand in shallow water in search of worms and other small creatures. Common Auger usually found near Acorn Worm burrows, suggesting that these worms are its only prey. Some augers immobilize their victim with a mild poison.

In sand. Low tide to shallow waters 100ft. deep. Virginia to Florida; Gulf of Mexico to Texas; West Indies. A common shell washed up on southern beaches.

Dana's and San Pedro Augers: W. coast, S. Los Angeles to S. Baja Cal. Other augers in Gulf of Mexico. Other tall pointed shells include Turret Shells, Ceriths and Wentletraps.

71

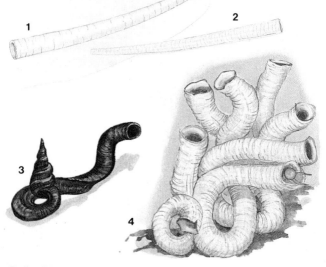

Indian Money Tusk (**1**) 2in. Shell a simple tube open both ends, white, slightly curved & tapering. Lie buried head-down in sand with only open apex projecting above surface (vents waste water.) Cone-shaped foot used for burrowing & anchorage. Feeds on microscopic forams & other animals. Long thread-like tentacles ending in sticky knobs extend into sand to catch prey. Sand & mud in waters 6–500ft. deep. Alas.–S. Cal. Used by Indians for ornament & currency.

Ivory Tusk (**2**) 2½in., is thinner. N.C., G. Mex.–Tex. & W.I.

Common Worm Shell (**3**) 1–4in. Like an uncoiled auger, coiled apex but subsequent whorls more uncoiled. Yellowish to red-brown. Subtidal with sponges & other colonial animals. Often cast ashore, may be broken. S.E. Fla. & W.I.; also S. New England.

Scaled Worm Shell (**4**) Forms large twisted masses of grayish white tubes each up to ½in. wide, 7in. long. Secretes mucous net to catch plankton. On rocks, shells, pilings at low tide. Monterey, Cal.–Mex. Above Point Conception, C. Cal., occur as individuals rather than masses.

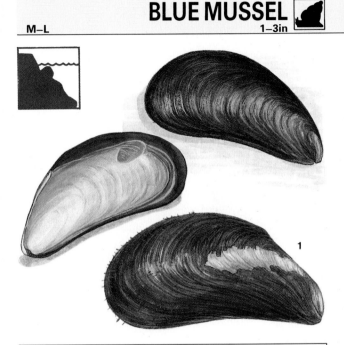

Elongated, curved, fan-shaped valves. Smooth blue-black with shiny periostracum. Concentric growth rings and shell often eroded near pointed terminal beaks. Pearly white inside with blue border and oval muscle scar. Long ligament, tiny indistinguishable teeth.

Mussels secrete strong horny byssal threads to attach themselves to substrate. Small probe-like foot secretes byssus, attaches threads to suitable hard objects, often in fan-like pattern. Filter feeders, withstand long exposure.

On pilings, stones and rocks in estuaries, rocks on more exposed coasts. Often in extensive beds with barnacles. Mid- to low tide; Arctic to South Carolina; Alaska to Baja California. Edible.

Northern Horse Mussel (1:) 2–6in. Periostracum shaggy. Beaks sub-terminal. Low tide; Arc.–N.J.; Alas.–S. Cal. Californian Mussel: 2–10in.; purplish gray; rayed. Alas.–Mex.

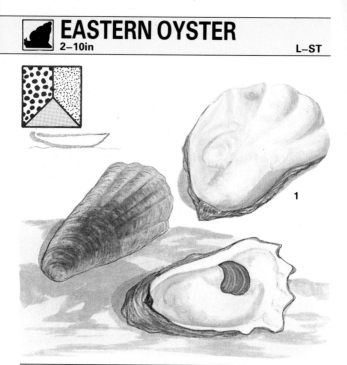

Heavy, irregular, dirty gray shell, valves unequal in size. Lower (left) valve shallow, dish-like, cemented to hard substrate. Upper (right) valve smaller, forms a flat lid. White inside with a single purplish muscle scar.

Form large beds in brackish sounds and estuaries. Die if exposed to fresh- or open seawater for too long. Edible and commercially harvested on east coast, in particular New York, New Jersey and Connecticut. Hand picked or dredged.

Abundant on sand, mud and gravel in brackish water, low tide to 40ft. deep. Gulf of St. Lawrence to Florida, Texas, Bahamas and West Indies. Introduced to California.

Native Pacific Oyster (1:) 2–3in. Oval, irregular. Muscle scar same color as shell interior. S. Alas.–Baja Cal. Edible, but Giant Pacific Oyster (12in.) now main commercial species.

Giant Atlantic Cockle (**1**) 3–4in. Plump, heart-shaped, equal valves, each with 35 strong radial ribs. Pale yellow, red-brown streaks, brown at margin. Pink-orange & white inside. Foot dark red. 2 frilly siphons. Burrow into mud & sand, often until only siphons exposed at surface. 1 siphon draws water into shell, gills extract oxygen & food particles. Other vents waste water. Largest American cockle, edible. Low tide to 100ft. Va.–N. Fla., Tex., Mex. Other cockles smaller & generally more northern in distribution.

Atlantic Bay Scallop (**2**) 2–3in. Inflated round shell, deeper lower valve, 17–18 strong ribs, hinge formed by 2 almost equal wings. Variable gray, yellowish, brown to reddish. Lower valve pale, may be white. Mantle edge between valves tentacled, has 30–40 bright blue eyes. Reacts to movement by clapping valves & swimming away. On sand & mud, often in eelgrass beds. N.S.–N. Fla. & Tex. Caught commercially but now overfished. Atlantic Deep-sea Scallop sold in markets. Other small scallops are attractive beach shells.

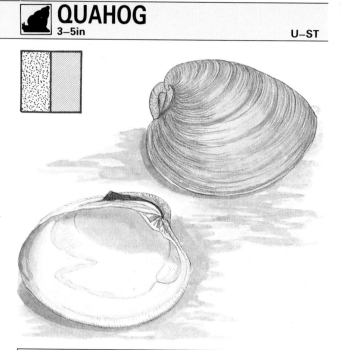

Thick, strong, rounded shell with forward-pointing beaks. Whitish, gray to tan with many concentric growth lines; sharp ridges when young, older clams smooth in central area. Inside white with purple stain at rear. Prominent teeth, ligament, 2 muscle scars and adjoining pallial sinus (s-line.)

Used commercially for chowders under several regional names. Young clams up to 2in. are "Cherrystones," for clambakes. "Chowder" clams are over 3in. Live for weeks out of water if kept cool, since valves remain tightly closed.

Found in mud and sand from high to low tide and in shallow water. Gulf of St. Lawrence to Florida and Texas. Introduced into California, but not common.

Southern Quahog: 6in.; more inflated. Older specimens not smooth in middle of shell; inside rarely purple. Ches. Bay–Tex. The 2 clams hybridize, difficult to distinguish. See also **Black Clam**.

Surf Clam (**1**) 4–7in. Heavy smooth shell with tan periostracum. Beaks just off center, fine growth lines, rear gape for siphons. Hinge with chondrophore & lateral teeth. In clean sand, low to subtidal, cast up after winter storms. N.S.– S.C. Other species E. & W. coasts.

Black Clam (**2**) 2–5in. Like **Quahog**, but covered in thick brown periostracum & pallial line not indented to form sinus. Sand & mud, subtidal. Nfld.–C. Cod, offshore S. to N.C. Common beach shell N. of C. Cod.

Soft-shelled Clam (**3**) 3–4in. (6in.) Valves gape both ends. Grayish, thin periostracum, rough surface, wrinkled growth lines. Chondrophore on left hinge, right has heart-shaped pit, lateral teeth weak. Burrows to 10in., siphons reach surface. Sand & mud, low-subtidal. Arc.–S.C.; Alas.–Cal.

Pacific Gaper (**4**) 5½–7½in. Large gape at front. Yellowish white, brown flaky periostracum. Irregular growth lines. Interior white, teeth weak, very large pallial sinus. Burrows to 1–3ft. in sand & sandy mud. Low to subtidal. Siphons reach surface. Edible. Puget Sound– Baja Cal.

Tellins & macomas are similar in appearance & habit. Flattened, oval, move rapidly in sand or mud. Not suspension feeders but suck up detritus with snake-like inhalant siphon.

Salmon Tellin (1) ¾in. Pinkish. Low tide sand. Alas.–S. Cal. Baltic Macoma. 1½in., grayish. Ga.–Arc. in mud.

Coquina (2) ½–1in. Brightly colored, wedge shells, banded or plain. Valves remain joined. In surf zone of exposed sandy beaches, mid-low tide. Move with tide & burrow rapidly if exposed between waves. Edible. Del.–Tex., less common N. of C. Hatt.

Common Razor Clam (3) 8in. Long, parallel sides & square gaping ends. Smooth, with olive-tan periostracum, fine growth lines. Deep burrows in sand, low tide. Lab.–Ga. Edible. Similar species on E. & W. coasts.

BORING CLAMS

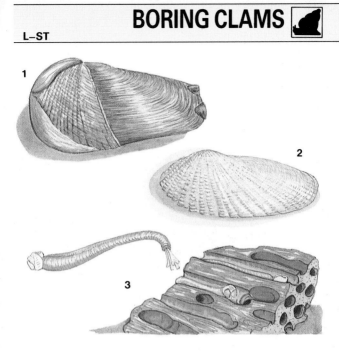

Flat-tipped Piddock (**1**) 3in. White, gaping front file-like with ridges & plates. Diagonal groove and flatter rear. 1 long tooth, siphons joined. Drills cylindrical holes in clay, peat, cement or sandstone. Low tide to 300ft. Alas.–Baja Cal.

False Anglewing (**2**) 2in. White, piddock-like, but no calcareous plates, clam-like teeth. Gray siphons, separate. In soft rocks on sheltered coasts. Low tide & below. G. St. Law.–G. Mex.; San Fran. Bay & C. Wash. True anglewings have stronger ribs & spoon-like plate on beak.

Common Shipworm (**3**) 12in. or more. Yellowish, worm-like. Reduced shell (¼in.) drills into wood. Valves white, sharp & ridged at front. Body fills tunnel, mantle secretes chalky deposit to line walls. 2 siphons open at entrance. Worldwide in wood; submerged but not buried. Nfld.–Fla., Tex., W.I. California Pacific Shipworm: larger, body to 39in., shell ½in. Alas.–Baja Cal. Both low tide & below in almost any untreated wood. Often numerous. Pest of wharves, pilings, wooden boats.

Pink, orange, tan, cream, gray, greenish, bluish to purple in color. 5 long arms taper to narrow tips, each with a red eye spot. Body is soft and flabby, usually with a row of spines down the middle of each arm. Underside of each arm bears 4 rows of tube feet in a groove which radiates from the central mouth.

Use powerful arms to surround and force open shells of clams and mussels just enough to insert their stomach and digest prey. Flexible tube feet tipped with suction cups cling to rocks or shell of prey. Can usually regenerate lost arms.

On rock or gravel bottoms, between high and low tide, and in shallow waters to 1145ft. deep. Atlantic coast from Labrador to Cape Hatteras. Large numbers may be seen on mussel beds, particularly in New England.

Ochre Star: rows of white spines; Alas.–Baja Cal. Forbes Common Sea Star: firm skeleton, more spiny; Me.–Tex. **Giant Sea Star:** long blunt spines surrounded by blue rings; B. Col.–Cal.

Slender Sea Star (**1**) Radius 3–4in. Bluish or salmon-brownish, fine dark line down each arm. Central disk small. 5 narrow arms, covered with blocks of small brush-like spines. Burrow in sand & mud, subtidal. Often washed ashore. E. Va.–Brazil. Rare N. to N.J.

Cushion Star (**2**) Radius to 10in. Plump with 5 short arms. Reddish, brown, orange or yellowish, network pattern in contrasting color. Olive green young. Firm hard skeleton, short spines. Dried as souvenirs. Subtidal, on sand, coral & rubble. N.C.–Fla., W.I.–Bra.

Spiny Sun Star (**3**) Radius 7in. 10–12 arms, large central disk. Scarlet with red, pink, whitish bands. Upper surface bristly. Feed on smaller sea stars. On rocky substrates, low tide to 1000ft. Arc.–G.Me.; Alas. to Puget Sound.

Blood Star (**4**) Radius 2–4in. Upper surface granular, red, orange or purple, whitish. Underside white. Small central disk, 5 long arms cylindrical with red eyespot at tip. Filter feeder. Rocky bottoms from low tide to deep waters. Arc.–C. Hatt. Pacific Blood Star: similar; Alas.–Baja Cal.

81

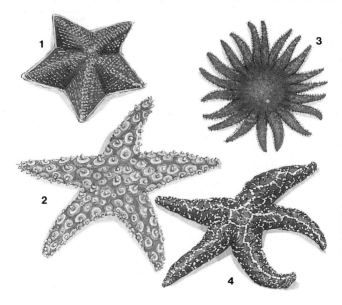

Bat Star (**1**) Radius 4in. 5 short arms, webbed between, scaly. Variable color: red, orange, brown, yellow, green, purple, often mottled. A small worm, *Ophiodromus pugettensis*, lives in grooves. Eats sea stars, sea squirts & algae. Protected rocky areas & on sand, low tide to 950ft. Alas.–Baja Cal.

Giant Sea Star (**2**) Radius 12in. Thick heavy arms. Bluish gray, sometimes with red, brown or purple. Blunt club-shaped spines surrounded at base by ring of blue flesh. On rocky shores, low-subtidal. B. Col.–Mex.

Sunflower Star (**3**) At least 16in. dia. Juveniles have 6 arms, increasing to 15–24. Central disk wide, arms, limp & flexible with soft fleshy covering, break off easily. Orange, purple to pink. Moves rapidly. Feeds on urchins, clams & dead fish. Rocky & soft bottoms. Low-subtidal. Alas. to Monterey.

Ochre Star (**4**) Radius 10in. Heavy, rough, purple, red, brown or ochre. Rows of white-tipped spines in a net-like pattern, form a pentagon on central disk. Feeds on mussel beds, barnacles, limpets, snails. Mid to low tide. Alas.–Mex.

DAISY BRITTLE STAR ✶

disk ¾in dia.; arms 3in long

Rounded, flattened disk distinct from 5 slender, jointed arms.
Color red to yellow, pink, white, bluish to black, green, brown,
variously spotted, banded and mottled. Central disk lobed
between arms covered with tiny spines and plates. Arms spiny.
Mouth at base of arms on lower surface of disk.

Mobile, rapidly seek new refuge when uncovered. Arms have
snake-like movement (also called "serpent stars",) but break
easily when handled, hence "brittle." Feed on bottom detritus,
small animals and carrion. Can regenerate lost arms.

Exposed or hidden under rocks in tide pools, among kelp
holdfasts, often on red algae. Often in areas of strong tidal
currents, waves. Lower shore to 5400ft. deep. Arc. to Cape Cod
(rarely to Long Island Sound;) Alaska to S. Cal.

Spiny Brittle Star: disk ¾in. diam., arms 6in. Long thorny spines
on arms and disk. Very agile, drops arms easily. Mid to low tide.
C. Cal. to Peru. Similar Atlantic species in east.

Skeleton of calcareous plates form a rigid globular test. This is covered with short (¾in.,) round-ended movable spines which bear ridges along their length. Green to olive. Spines sometimes reddish with pale tips.

Anus located centrally on top of test, surrounded by small scaly plates. 5 rows of plates bearing tube feet radiate from this area to mouth under the test. Mouth has 5 chewing teeth. Graze on algae. May live in shallow holes bored into rocks.

On rocks and among seaweeds from low tide to 3700ft. deep. Often in large numbers. Alaska to Puget Sound and Washington. Arctic to Cape Cod, extending to New Jersey offshore. The most common urchin in New England tidepools.

Purple Urchin: 4in. dia. Red to purple, juveniles greenish, like Green Urchin. Numerous on exposed coasts; burrow into rocks. Lower shore; Alaska to Mexico.

OTHER URCHINS ★

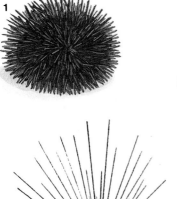

Red Urchin (1) 5in. dia. Wine-red, or brownish-purple. Spines pale to reddish black, to 3in. Does not burrow. Alas.–Mex. Quiet & exposed rocky coasts. In Cal., in shallow water (kelp beds,) or tide pools. Eaten by sea otters.

Long-spined Urchin (2) 4in. dia., with long slender spines (8–12in.) Purple to black, young speckled white. Urchin aims all spines towards nearby movement. **CAUTION**: spines penetrate deeply, difficult & painful to remove. Low-subtidal, on coral reefs, rocks, pools. Fla., Ber., W.I., Mex.–Sur.

Heart Urchin (3) 2in. long, heart-shaped, mud colored, with 5 deep grooves. Lipped mouth at front of lower surface, anus at rear. Short fine spines, longer beneath. Dead tests white, fragile. Buried in mud & sand. Low tide. C. Hatt.–Tex., W.I. Other W. coast species.

Sand Dollar (4) Flat, 3in. dia., ¼in. high. Brownish, purple to red, short fine spines. Dead test white. 5-petalled pattern on upper surface, mouth central beneath, anus at rear. In loose sand. Lab.–Md., Alas.–Puget Sound. Similar species S.E. & S.W.

85

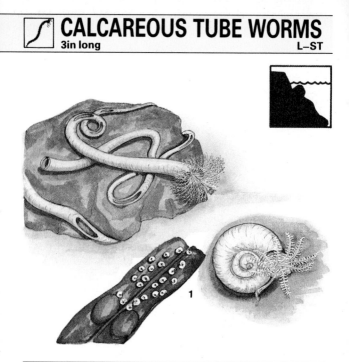

1

Species of *Hydroides*. Secrete white calcareous, cylindrical tubes, often twisted, spiralled and ridged. Translucent green body, short thorax, longer abdomen. Branchial crown of 15–20 filaments, often mottled red, yellow or white. 1 filament forms plug-like operculum. Tubes solitary or tangled.

Branchial crown extended in water as gills and filter feeding structure. Rapidly withdraws into tube if disturbed. Operculum seals the aperture. Opercular shape varies with species and is often elaborately sculptured.

Tubes firmly attached to any hard object, from low tide to waters 50ft. deep. On rocks, stones and shells cast ashore by storms. Cosmopolitan fouling species on boats, buoys, harbors, etc.

Sinistral Spiral Tube Worm (1:) white, snail-like tube, coiled clockwise, ⅛in. in diameter. Abundant on rock weeds and kelp. Pacific; Maine to Cape Cod. Similar species also on rocks.

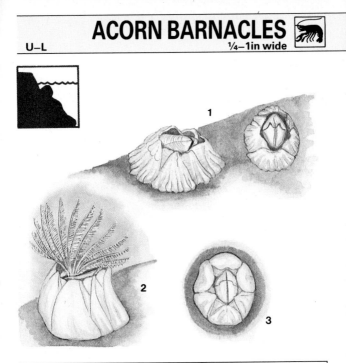

Several similar species on east, west and Gulf coasts. Crustaceans with jointed legs, but bodies enclosed by shell of 6 chalky plates which are firmly stuck to rocks, pilings, ships etc. Diamond-shaped "trapdoors" closed by 2 pairs of plates. Shell form variable.

Shrimp-like animal stands on its head with legs extended through "trapdoor," which opens in water (even wave splashes.) 6 pairs of feathery legs comb water for food particles and respiration. Free-swimming larvae later settle with adults.

On rocks and hard substrates. **Northern Rock Barnacle** (1:) ½in. Crowded. High to low tide; Arc.–Del. **Ivory Barnacle** (2:) 1in. Estuaries; high-subtidal; Me.–S. Am. **Little Gray Barnacle** (3:) ⅜in. High tide, above (1) and (2;) C. Cod to Fla., Tex., W.I.

Acorn Barnacle: similar to (1;) ¾in.; high-mid tide; Alas.–Mex. Dall's Barnacle: Alas.–S. Diego; Smooth Gray Barnacle: San Fran.–Mex. Both related to (3;) high tide above Acorn Barnacle.

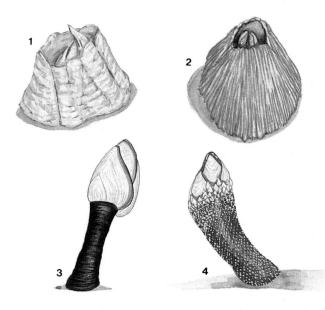

Giant Acorn Barnacle (1)
Large, 4in. wide. Aperture
large, flaring, trapdoor beaked.
Low to subtidal, on pilings &
rocks. Alas. to S. Cal. Eagle
Barnacle: similar but 5in. wide;
trapdoor plates have parallel
ridges; Cal., rare N. of S. Fran.
Volcano Barnacle (2) 2in. wide.
Volcano-shaped. Shell 4 plates,
margins concealed by deep
vertical furrows. Brick red.
Singly or in clusters on rocks,
exposed shores. High–low tide.
C.–Baja Cal., rare N. of S. Fran.
West Indian Volcano Barnacle:
whitish to dark gray. Fla. Keys–
W.I.

Goose Barnacle (3) 6in.
Flattened, bluish white plates,
with purple & yellowish
margins. On leathery stalk,
slightly retractible. 6 pairs of
feathery legs comb water for
food. Floats on surface attached
to any drifting object, often cast
ashore. Floating Goose Barnacle:
secretes gas-filled float. Both all
coasts.
Leaf Barnacle (4) 4in. tall. On
rocks of exposed coasts, midtide.
6 large white plates & many
overlapping smaller ones also on
wrinkled stalk. Form dense
stands in mussel beds. B. Col. to
Mexico.

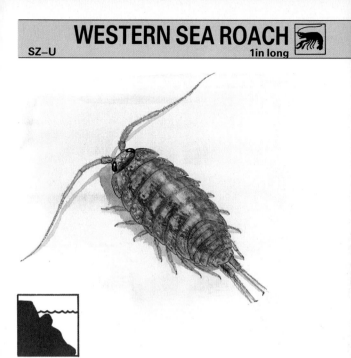

Resemble sow bugs. Oval, flattened, tan to gray, mottled with pale dots. Paler at night, dark during day. Eyes black. Rough texture. Large antennae. 7 pairs of legs. Tail divides into 2 appendages which divide again into 2 long points, at least ⅓ of body length.

An isopod found on and under stones and rocks at high tide level. May be very abundant locally. Particularly active at night, hide in crevices by day. Run fast if disturbed to seek new refuge. Terrestrial sow bugs inhabit debris above beach.

In crevices on rocks and jetties at high tide level and above. Central California to Central America.

Exotic Sea Roach: 1¼in. Tail appendages ½ body length; Chesapeake Bay to Florida, W.I. Northern Sea Roach: 1in. Tail appendages ¼ body length. North of Massachusetts Bay.

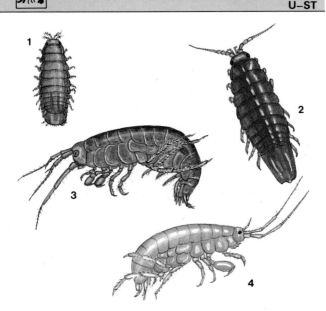

Gribble (1) ³⁄₁₆in. Wood-boring isopod. Rolls into ball when exposed. Burrows, ¹⁄₁₆in. dia., run with grain of wood. In pilings & driftwood, low to subtidal.

Baltic Isopod (2) 1in. Large squarish tail shield. Variable: tan, green, red-black, plain, mottled, banded, or striped. On seaweeds or in pools, lower shore. G. St. Law.–N.C. Other species W. & E.

Scud (3) 1in. Olive to red. Arched back, kidney-shaped eyes. 2 pairs long antennae, 7 pairs walking legs: 1 & 2 with large claw, 5–7 bent back. In rockweeds, crevices & pools.

Swim on sides. Mid-low shore. Arc.–Ches. Bay. Other species, W. & E., fresh & salt water.

Beach Fleas: ¾–1¼in. On sand, high tide mark & above. Arched back, 7 pairs legs: large claw on 2nd, 6 & 7 bent back. Sandy gray to reddish-brown. Burrows in sand & under strand-line. At night & when disturbed, jump erratically into the air.

Long-horned Beach Flea (4:) long antennae. Large-eyed Beach Flea: large eyes. Both Nfld.–Fla. California Beach Flea: orange-red antennae. B.C.–S. Cal. Beach Fleas do not bite & eat only algae.

Head and thorax fused, covered by carapace bearing grooves and 10 teeth along mid-line, ending in short pointed rostrum between stalked eyes. Transparent gray to reddish-brown, often with dark spot on abdomen. Long antennae; 3 pairs of jointed mouthparts, 5 pairs of abdominal swimmerets; fan-like tail.

Basis of Atlantic shrimping industry, with similar Brown and White Shrimps. Boreal Red Shrimp are taken in winter. Bottom dwellers, they often burrow into sand. They escape with a sharp flick of the muscular abdomen.

On a variety of substrates from low tide to 200ft. From Caribbean north to Chesapeake Bay. Brown Shrimp north to Cape Cod; White Shrimp to Fire Island, N.Y.

Brown Shrimp: no abdominal spot. White Shrimp: short carapace grooves. Boreal Red Shrimp: 5in.; reddish; long rostrum; blunt spines on 3rd and 4th abdominal segments. Arc.–C. Cod. Edible.

Short, untoothed rostrum between eyes. One spine in middle of carapace. Heavy claw on first pair of walking legs. Transparent, colorless or mottled gray, brownish or black.

Scavengers, often eating dead fish and other animals. Abdominal swimmerets often used to brood eggs in females. Larvae are later free-swimming and planktonic. Shrimps are eaten by fish, anemones, crabs and man.

Common on sandy bottoms and eelgrass beds, also in estuaries. Low tide to 300ft. Arctic to E. Florida, but south of Cape Hatteras only inshore from January to June.

Common Shore Shrimp: 1½in. Toothed rostrum with forked tip; tidal pools; G. St. Law.–Yuc. Red Sand Shrimp: 5in. 3–4 teeth mid-carapace. Arc.–B. Fundy. Several similar W. species.

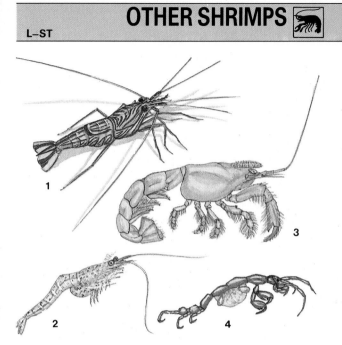

Red-lined Cleaning Shrimp (1)
2¾in. Translucent, red-striped.
Long toothed rostrum. Long
slender legs & antennae. Low to
subtidal. On rock, coral reefs,
jetties. Ches. Bay to Tex., W.I.–
Bra. Several related species
(Fla.–Carib.) beautifully
patterned. Often among sea
anemone tentacles, cleaning up
scraps of food.

Bent Opossum Shrimp (2) 1in.
Large eyes. Short carapace.
Bristly legs have 2 branches.
Pale yellowish with dark spots,
pinkish, notched tail. Near
seaweeds, rocks in pools &
subtidal. C. Cod–N.S.

Flat-browed Mud Shrimp (3) 2–
4in. Flat-topped, bristly
carapace, rounded rostrum. 1st
pair of legs with large bristly
claw. Blue-yellowish gray. In
pairs in U- or Y-shaped burrows
in sand & mud. C. Cod–Bra.
Bay Ghost Shrimp: 4½in.;
similar; white-pinkish; shorter
carapace; no rostrum; large,
broad hairless claws; high-mid
tide; S. Alas.–Baja Cal. Short-
browed Mud Shrimp: similar;
N.S.–Fla.

Skeleton Shrimp (4) ¾–2in.
Long, slender with mantis-like
claws, round head. Colorless,
red, greenish, tan. Among
seaweeds & hydroids. E. & W.

Shrimp-like, but flattened with a short carapace. Large stalked eyes and rounded antennal scales not covered by a rostrum. Pair of large mantis-like claws with 6 spines on a knife-like blade. 3 pairs of weak legs. Green or bluish, abdominal segments ridged with dark margins. Tail piece with blunt ridge.

Swim with looping motion, propelled by abdominal swimmerets; antennal scales are rudders. Feed on small fish and other small animals, caught by swift claws. Have punch of great force, easily fracture and lacerate: **HANDLE WITH CAUTION**.

Live in complex burrows with more than one exit in mud or sand. Low tide to waters 500ft. deep. Common but secretive; frequently caught in shrimp trawls. Cape Cod to Florida, Texas and Brazil.

Scaly-tailed Mantis: 12in. 8–11 spines on claw. Fla.–Tex.; W.I.–Brazil. **CAUTION**. Other smaller species, 1–4in. long, have 0, 4 and 10 spines on claw. S.E. coasts and Caribbean.

Cylindrical body with 5 pairs of walking legs. First pair has massive pincers, unequal in size: left usually large and blunt, right smaller, sharp and pointed. Small pincers on 2nd and 3rd legs. Green-black, bluish or brown, pale beneath. Tips of appendages reddish. 1 pair of antennae longer than body.

Scavengers, feed on carrion and algae. Large claw used to crack shells and other hard objects. Fished commercially and considered by I.U.C.N. (1988) to be under threat of extinction unless their exploitation is regulated. Turn red when boiled.

Among rocks in crevices and caves, shallow water (10ft. deep) to edge of continental shelf. Will tolerate estuarine waters. Labrador to Virginia. **CAUTION!** Avoid pincers and snapping tail.

Spiny and Rock Lobsters are generally red or brownish and lack large pincers. **Spanish Lobster** is squat and lacks both large pincers and long antennae.

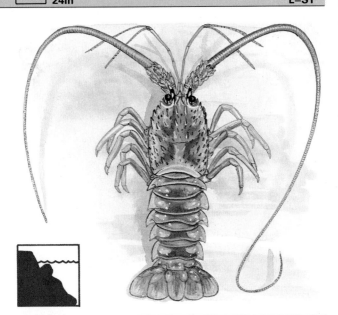

Cylindrical body with spiny carapace; 2 longest spines above eyes. Abdominal segments smooth but furrowed. No pincers on walking legs (females have tiny claws on last pair.) 2nd pair of antennae spiny, stout, longer than body. Tan with gray, green, white, purplish hues, paler beneath. Legs bluish.

Secretive, nocturnal, hiding by day. Heavily fished and no longer abundant. Lobsters are caught in baited traps (pots) which they enter as a retreat. **CAUTION**: spines can cause deep wounds if animal is mishandled. Strong muscular tail snaps.

In crevices among rocks and reefs from low tide to waters 300ft. deep. Cape Hatteras to Florida and Gulf of Mexico, Bermuda, West Indies and Brazil. Locally, may be known as "crawfish."

California Rock Lobster: 16in. Red, tan-orange with red spines; legs brownish. Abdominal segments bumpy. Low to subtidal in pools. C. Cal. to Baja Cal. Caught commercially.

Spanish Lobster (**1**) broad; bumpy carapace, antennae shovel-like. Yellow to red brown, mottled. 4 spots on 1st abdominal segment. **Horseshoe Crab** (**2**) tan, horseshoe-shaped carapace, two eyes. Triangular tailpiece, marginal spines, spine-like tail. 5 pairs walking legs and book gills beneath.

Both push through soft sediments eating worms and other creatures. (**1**) edible. (**2**) primitive arthropod, little changed since prehistoric times. 3 nights at full moon in spring, migrate inshore to lay eggs in sand.

(**1**) sand and shelly bottoms, coral reefs. Shallow waters, S. Fla., W.I., Bahamas. (**2**) mud and sand. Lower shore to shallow water 75ft. deep. Often seen on bottom in shallow water from jetties and wharves. Bar Harbor, Me. to Gulf of Mexico.

(**1**) Ridged Slipper Lobster: similar; up to 5in. long; lacks 4 abdominal spots; on mud, sand, shell, grassy beds, coral reefs N.C. to Fla., Tex., W.I., Bermuda. (**2**) no similar species.

Rounded body and 5 pairs of long spidery legs, up to 6in. long in male. 1st pair end in small pincers. Carapace covered in spines and hooked hairs, with 9 large spines down mid-line. Rostrum ends in V-shaped notch. Dull yellow to brown, usually coated with a variety of growth and debris.

Slow-moving bottom dweller. Carapace covered with algae (living and fragments,) hydroids, sponges, bryozoans, tubeworms, barnacles, dirt and debris, and blends into its surroundings. Harmless. Similar species eaten in Europe.

Found on all substrates. Low tide to at least 160ft. Nova Scotia to Gulf of Mexico as far as Texas.

Doubtful Spider Crab: deep "V" rostrum. B. Fundy to Tex., Bah., Cuba. Masking Crab: 5–6in. legs; camouflaged with numerous encrusting animals and algae. N. California to Mexico.

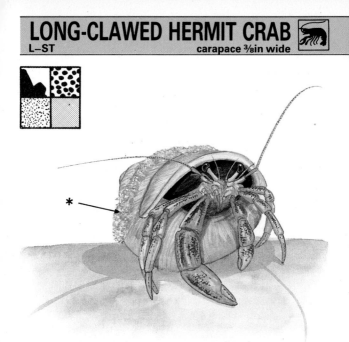

*

Lives in snail shell carried to protect soft-skinned abdomen, coiled to fit shell. 3 pairs of walking legs protrude from shell, 1st pair with pincers. Right pincer larger, elongate, smooth or slightly grainy. Stalked eyes. Long antennae. Gray to greenish white. Often with dark stripe on large claw.

Although difficult for predators to remove, leave shells easily and try new shells to find perfect fit. Seek progressively larger shells. 5 pairs of legs, last 2 reduced within shell. Shells often covered with **Snail Fur (★,)** a hydroid colony.

On various substrates, sand, mud, rocky tide pools and in estuaries. Low tide to shallow waters 150ft. deep. Massachusetts Bay to Florida and Texas. Also locally to Nova Scotia in warmer bays.

Many E. and W. coast species; claws: broad, hairy, flat, striped. Blue-handed Hermit: blue legs and white bands; broad, blue pincers. Mid-low shore; Alas. to Baja Cal.

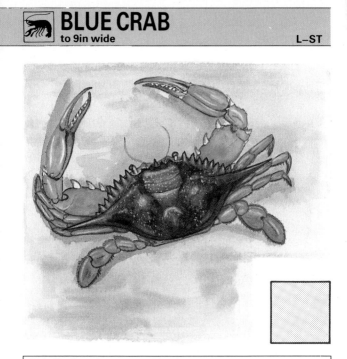

Spindle-shaped carapace, width 2½ times length, 2 long spines at widest point. Female rounded. 8 marginal teeth, 4 bumps between eyes. Olive to bluish above, white below. 4 pairs of walking legs, last with swimming paddle. Powerful elongate pincer ribbed, bright blue below. 3 spines on upper arm.

On mud, feeding on vegetation and carrion. In estuaries, may range to fresh waters. Migrates to deep waters in winter. Caught with trap and line and trawled from deep water. Main commercial species on E. coast. **Aggressive**: may bite.

Common in estuaries and offshore. Low tide to 120ft. In shallow water in summer, often clinging to wharves and pilings. Cape Cod (occasionally north to Massachusetts Bay) to Uruguay. Gulf of Mexico as far as Texas.

A closely related crab, *Callinectes similis*, 5in. wide, has only 2 teeth between eyes; south of Cape May. Speckled Crab, 4½in. wide, is brown with white spots; south of Cape Cod.

Carapace 1½ times as wide as long, with 5 pointed marginal teeth and 3 between eyes. Powerful pincers of equal, moderate size. 4 pairs walking legs, last pair flattened, but pointed. Greenish, mottled black and yellow above, paler yellowish below. Females orange-red below.

Introduced from N. Europe, now most common shore crab in New England. Throws off legs to escape predators, (seagulls.) Tolerates low salinities. Tail, 5-jointed in male, 7-jointed in female, tucked tight under abdomen.

Most shores: sand, rocks, gravel, mud. Mid to lower shore and shallow waters. Open coastlines to upper estuaries. Often under stones, algae, debris, tidal pools, crevices, in and around wharves and jetties. Nova Scotia to Manasquan Inlet, N.J.

Lady Crab: carapace 3in. wide; 5 sharp marginal teeth, 3 between eyes. Gray, clustered purple spots. 5th leg, swimming paddle. **Aggressive**. Low tide; Cape Cod to Gulf of Mexico.

Generally flattened. Carapace squarish, smooth with 3 marginal teeth. Eyes large, wide apart with no teeth between. Wine to purplish black, may be greenish. Pale beneath. Large equal pincers, purple-reddish with darker spots. Walking legs flattened, with pointed tips.

The dominant mid-tide crab of the West coast. Feeds on algal films coating rocks and other substrates, but will also take carrion. Sluggish. Young are difficult to distinguish from the Yellow Shore Crab.

Amongst seaweeds at mid-tide level on sheltered rocky shores. Prefers coarse sand and gravel with overlying rocks. Locally abundant from Sitka to Mexico.

Lined Shore Crab: 2¼in.; eyes far apart; blackish, pale lines; Ore.–Mex. Yellow Shore Crab: 1⅜in.; yellowish; muddy sand; Alas.–Baja Cal. Mottled Shore Crab: ½in.; N.C.–G. Mex.

Oval carapace with 9 blunt marginal teeth forming pie-crust edge.
3 teeth between eyes. Yellowish, speckled with red-purple brown
spots. Whitish beneath. Heavy pincers have black tips. Legs short
with hairy edges, pointed tips.

This and **Green Crab** are commonest New England shore crabs.
Easily found in crevices and under rocks, jetties. Often buried in
sand with just the eyes exposed. Edible, caught in lobster pots.

Rocky shores, sand and gravel, lower estuaries. Low tide to
2600ft.; Labrador to South Carolina. More subtidal south of Cape
Cod.

Jonah Crab: 6¼in.; rounded shell; 9 jagged marginal teeth; N.S.–
Fla. Pacific Rock Crab: 11 marginal teeth; Ore.–Mex. Dungeness
Crab: 9¼in.; pincers not black-tipped; fished; Alas.–S. Cal.

103

Males have one claw greatly enlarged (1⅝in. long.) Claws bluish or red brown; fingertips whitish; inner palm smooth, outer bumpy. Female claws small and equal. Carapace squarish, no marginal teeth, purple to brown or grayish, mottled with purple patch. Eyes on long stalks.

In colonial burrows, up to 12in. deep. Small balls of excavated sand carried to surface. Eats algal film on sand grains. Large pincer used for semaphore-like signals in courtship. Harmless, but legs easily damaged if roughly handled. Often numerous.

High on sheltered beaches, creeks and coastal marshes. Boston Harbor to Florida and West Indies; Gulf of Mexico to Texas. Common.

Mud Fiddler: 1in.; tubercles on claw palm; estuaries, mud, C. Cod–Fla.; Fla.–Tex. Brackish Water Fiddler: 1½in.; claw joints red; C. Cod–Tex. California. Fiddler: ¾in.; S.–Baja Cal.

Shell squarish, no marginal teeth, gritty surface, H-shaped depression. Sandy to grayish white. Large club-shaped eyestalks longer than space between eyes. Pincers unequal, toothed. Strong, hairy walking legs.

Burrow into sand dunes, up to 4ft. down, to reach moisture. Rush into surf for scraps and to wet gills; drown if kept submerged. Active at night and on cloudy afternoons, run out of burrows and disappear down others. Inquisitive.

Burrows on seaward side of sand dunes, young nearest to high tide mark. If quietly observed, hundreds may be visible running over the beach. Cape Henlopen, Delaware to Florida and Texas: West Indies to Brazil.

Female **Fiddler Crab** similar. Marsh Crab: 1⅛in. wide; dark olive; eyestalks short, space between greater than length; intertidal on salt marshes, mud; Cape Cod to Texas.

105

Kelp Crab (**1**) Shield-like 4in. carapace beaked. Aggressive: **BEWARE** claws. On kelp, low rocky shore. Alas.–Mex.

Land Crab (**2**) Globular 5in. carapace. Blue-gray or white. 1 pincer large. In estuarine mud, mangroves. S. Fla.–Tex. Edible.

Flat Porcelain Crab (**3**) ⁷⁄₈in., flattened. 5th pair legs folded under body. Mid tide. B.Col.–S. Cal. Other species E. & W.

Commensal Crabs (**4**) ⁵⁄₈in. Pea-like or oval. In clams or other creatures. Soft shell. E. & W.

Mole Crab (**5**) 1in. long, egg-shaped. Exposed beaches. Good bait. Similar species E. & W. Spiny Mole Crab 2⅜in. C. & S. Cal. **Shamefaced Crab** (**6**) 5½in. wide. Hides face behind deep, sculptured pincers. Shallow water. G. Mex.–Fla. Occ N. to C. Hatt. Dolly Varden has spotted back. Ches. Bay–G. Mex. **Black-clawed Mud Crabs** (**7**) ⁷⁄₈–1½in. Several species W. & E.–Gulf coasts. Under rocks on mud & sand.

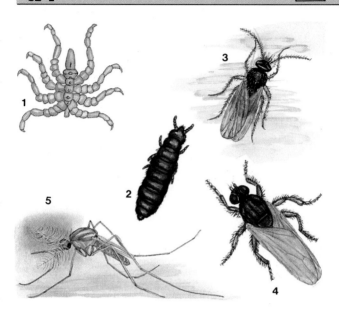

Anemone Sea Spider (**1**) ½in. long. Louse-like. Small body, 4 pairs stout clawed legs. Feed on anemones. Under rocks, low tide. G. St. Law.–L.I. Sound. Stearn's Sea Spider similar; B. Col.–C. Cal.

Intertidal insects include: **Seashore Springtail** (**2**) ¹⁄₁₆–⅛in. long. Simple, no wings. Plump, dark blue-gray. Among debris or floating raft-like on surface of tidal pools. All coasts. **Sand Flies** (Punkies) (**3**) ¹⁄₁₆–⅛in. Cause itchy **bites**. Larvae in salt marshes & sand. W., S. & E. coasts.

Seaweed Flies (**4**) ⅛–⅜in. Blackish, flattened, bristly legs. Swarm over decaying seaweeds where eggs laid. Separate E. & W. coast species. Arc.–R.I.; S. Alas.–N. Cal. **Salt Marsh Mosquitos:** ⅛–¼in. Female **bites**. Feathery antennae on male. Larvae in brackish & saltwater, also swimming pools. **Golden Salt Marsh Mosquito** (**5**) N.B.–Fla. & Tex. Black & white species from Mass. through Fla. to G. Mex. & S. Cal.

Many terrestrial insects also stray into tidal zones.

107

Color variable: bright green to reddish brown with lavender or pink. 4–6 saddle-like markings on back, with paler circles below. Fins spiny with darker bands on all except pelvics. Blunt spines on operculum, eyes high on head. Short hair-like cirri on head and lateral line.

Sculpins are a large group of generally small fish occurring in fresh and marine waters. The related Cabezon may be seen in shallow waters, Alaska to Baja California and grows up to 3 feet. Edible and prized by anglers, its eggs are **poisonous**.

Under rocks and in tidal pools from high to low tide and on reefs in shallow waters. Alaska to Mexico.

There are many similar sculpins on the west coast, with frequently overlapping distribution.

MOLLY MILLER

Short blunt head and elongated body, deepest behind head, then tapering to tail. Olive green with dark blotches and pearly spots. No scales. Long continuous dorsal fin, broad spiny pectoral fins. Eyes are large and set high on the head. Small mouth with large fleshy lips. Row of cirri on top of head.

Like many shallow water bottom-dwelling fish, the Molly Miller has strong spiny pectoral fins which brace it against currents between stones and crevices. Feeds mainly on plant material.

In sandy tide pools, or between rocks and around jetties. Lower shore and shallow water. Florida to Gulf of Mexico, Bermuda, Brazil.

Several similar blennies occur on East and Gulf coasts. Feather Blenny: 4in; in shallow waters over mud and oyster beds; blue spot on male's dorsal fin. Nova Scotia, Gulf of Mexico to Mex.

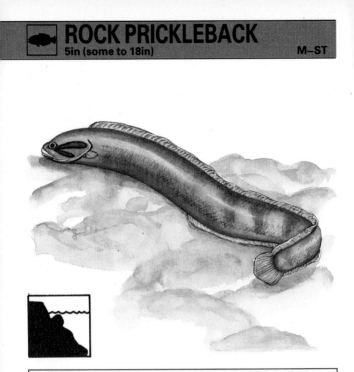

Long, eel-like fishes, greenish gray to greenish black. Two dark bars behind each eye, eyes positioned high on head. Fleshy lips. Long dorsal fin starts just above operculum, anal fin about halfway down body, both continuous. Squarish tail.

Bottom dwellers, hiding under boulders and in crevices. Eat small fish, crustaceans, sponges and algae. Females larger than males. Spawn in winter, eggs attached to rocks.

Rocky shores, mid to low tide and down to 80ft. Under rocks and in pools. Port San Juan, Alaska to Point Arguello, California.

Monkeyface Prickleback: to 30in.; light to dark brown, two fleshy bumps on top of head. Ore. to Baja Cal. Penpoint Gunnel: to 18in.; yellowish. Alaska to S. California.

Short head, elongate, tapering, cylindrical body. Tan to olive, mottled brown with large scales. Two dorsal fins, first black-edged, second long, almost to rounded tail fin. Pectoral fins not obviously spiny, joined beneath to form suction disk. Eyes high on head, iridescent blue mark beneath.

Large group of inshore fish. Spawn from April to October. Males guard eggs.

In bays and offshore, over mud and sand near reefs. Intertidal to waters 300ft. deep. British Columbia to Baja California.

Many similar species on east and west coasts. Sharptail Goby: 8in; brownish, long and thin with pointed tail and long spines on first dorsal fin. North Carolina to Mexico.

111

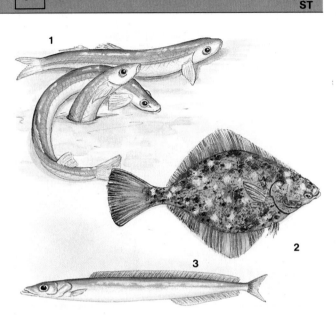

Californian Grunion (**1**) 5–7in. Cigar-shaped, greenish gray above, silver below & band down sides. Blunt nose, large eyes, first of 2 dorsal fins spiny. For 3–4 nights, Mar.–Sep., at full moon & high tide, masses of fish beach in pairs and slither to high tide mark. Female lays eggs in sand as fertilized by male. Edible & easily collected. Shallow waters off sandy beaches. San Francisco to Baja California.

Starry Flounder (**2**) 2in.–3ft. Flattened, diamond shaped. Lays on side with both eyes on right (uppermost) side. Variably mottled brown to black, underside white. Fins banded, scales rough, mouth small. On sand or mud in bays, upper estuaries, & offshore. Young in tide pools. Taken commercially. Alas.–C. Cal. Winter Flounder: 23in. Dorsal fin starts over eye. Lab.–Ches. Bay.

Sand Lance (**3**) 7in. Olive-bluish green, silvery below. Long dorsal fin. Large mouth, long lower jaw. Shallow water over sandy beaches, eel-like swimming motion or burrows into sand. N. Lab.–C. Hatt. Pacific Sand Lance, metallic blue. Alas.–L.A.

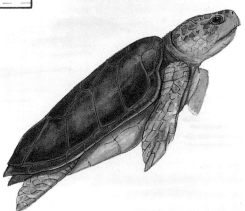

Carapace oval, keeled, reddish brown, with 5 plates on each side of back. Plates are smooth in adult, saw-toothed in young. Limbs paddle-like. Two pairs of scales between eyes. Powerful beak-like jaws.

Come inshore to breed and in search of food: clams, crabs, fish, seaweeds. Females drag themselves up onto sandy beaches to lay large clutches of eggs which lie buried in sand, until young hatch and return to the sea.

Ocean-going in southern Atlantic and Pacific oceans. Inshore on bays and estuaries. At night on breeding beaches, Texas to Virginia.

Green Turtle and Hawksbill: 4 plates each side of back. Atlantic Ridley: 30in; gray. Leatherback: 70in; black. All endangered species. Loggerhead considered vulnerable by IUCN.

113

HERRING GULL
23in

Common "seagull." Adult is white with pale gray back and wings. Wing tips are black with white spots. Heavy bill is yellow with a red spot, feet flesh-pink. Juveniles are mottled brown with darker wing and tail feathers and blackish bill. Adult plumage grows in the 3rd year.

Scavengers whose numbers are increasing. Search coastal areas and inland for food scraps, small animals, carrion, even berries. Drop shellfish to break open and trample sand to find worms. Nest in small colonies on cliffs, islands, rooftops.

Common along Atlantic, Pacific and Gulf coasts. Easily seen on beaches, estuaries and far inland on lakes, rivers, grassy fields and garbage dumps. Breed from Alaska to Greenland and south to North and South Carolina.

Ring-billed Gull: 18–20in.; yellow feet, black ring round bill. May be more numerous inland; forms very large nesting colonies. Alas. & Lab. to Gt. Lakes & Cal. Winters N. Eng. to Cuba.

LAUGHING GULL
15–17in

Adult has black head in summer; white with dark markings around eye and back of head in winter. Back and wings dark gray, blending into black wing tips; hind edge of wing white. Reddish black drooping bill. Legs dark red to black. Juveniles dark brown with white rump.

Named for its cry, a common summer gull on east and Gulf coasts, rare inland. Nests on the ground on sand and salt marshes; 3 dark mottled olive-brown eggs. Numbers declining due to destruction of habitat and competing **Herring Gulls**.

Bays, lagoons, salt marshes and estuaries. Rare inland. Feed on beaches and in harbors in winter. Maine to Caribbean, less frequent north of Virginia in winter.

Franklin's Gull: 13–15in; lives inland, but migrates to Gulf coast; white band separates black wing tip from gray.

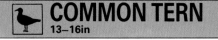

White with elongate black cap. Back and wings pale gray. Wings long with dark tips. Tail long and deeply forked. Red, black-tipped bill. Legs red to orange. In winter, black cap is reduced to a patch around the eye.

Fly low over water, head down looking for prey and plunge-dive for fish and crustaceans. Nest a shallow depression in sand or pebble beaches; 2–3 olive-buff spotted eggs. Attack humans if close to nesting colony.

Coastal beaches and islands, marshes, lakes and rivers. Labrador to Caribbean and inland, Wisconsin and Alberta to Labrador. Winter from Florida to South America, migrating south along east and west coasts.

Forster's Tern: 14–16in; wing tips frosty white; on marshes. Atlantic coast from Maryland to Texas; central and southern California coast. Inland, Alberta and California to Illinois.

Mottled rufous head and upper breast. Back grayish rufous and white. Belly white. In winter, light gray above, white below (illus.) Bill and legs black. Conspicuous white wing stripe visible in flight.

Breed on Arctic Ocean coasts, south to Hudson Bay. Sandy beaches of all coasts during winter. Rush after retreating surf to catch stranded tiny molluscs and crustaceans. Ground nest of grasses and lichens; 4 olive eggs have brown spots.

Sandy beaches, sandbars, less frequently mudflats. Dry stony arctic tundra in summer. Winter down east and west coasts to southern South America. Worldwide.

Several other similar Sandpipers. Dunlin: 8½in.; longer drooping bill; reddish back, white below, black belly. Winters from British Columbia to Mexico and New England to Florida and Mexico.

Ruddy Turnstone (**1**) 8–10in. Black bill, orange legs. Summer: back chestnut & black, head black & white, belly white, black breast band. Winter: dusky brown, white throat. Turns stones for food. Breeds Arc., winters S. from Cal. & N.C. Black Turnstone: black legs. Winters Alas.–Baja Cal.

Double-crested Cormorant (**2**) 30–35in. Slender body, long neck, hooked bill. Dark with orange throat patch. Tufts on head. Perch upright & spread wings. Eat fish. Coastal swamps, lakes & rivers; offshore islands. Alas.–Mex., Nfld.–Bah.

American Oystercatcher (**3**) 17–21in. Blackish brown, white belly & wing stripe. Pink feet. Stout red bill. Yellow eye. Eat clams & mussels on sand, pebbles, mud & salt marshes. Noisy courtship. S. from Baja Cal. & Mass.–S. America. Black Oystercatcher: black plumage; Alas.–Baja Cal.

Brant (**4**) 22–30in. Small marine goose. Back brown, short neck & head black, white cheek patch & belly. Breed on Arctic coastal tundra, winter in estuaries & bays, Vancouver Is.–Baja Cal; E. coast to N.C. Feed on eelgrass & other grasses.

A small seal with hind flippers turned backwards. Silver gray to brownish black, with or without dark spots. Creamy white beneath. No visible ears. Pups gray above, whitish below.

Offshore or basking on quiet beaches and low rocks. Bark when disturbed and retreat to water. Can stay underwater for 20 minutes. Feed on fish, squid and shellfish. One or, rarely, two pups born on land in early summer.

Often seen in shallow coastal waters, sheltered bays and coves, river mouths, estuaries, harbors. Arctic to Baja California; Arctic coast, Hudson Bay and Atlantic south to the Carolinas.

Californian Sea Lion: male to 8ft. Hind flippers turned forward on land. Buff to brown (look black when wet.) Small ears. Males bark. Rocky beaches, Vancouver Is. to Gulf of California.

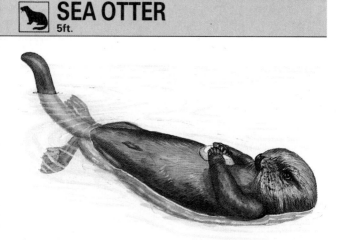

A large otter with dense, glossy, brownish black fur. White-tipped hairs give a frosted appearance. Head and neck yellowish gray. Feet fully webbed; hind feet flipper-like, forefeet small and hand-like. Stout tapering tail.

Feed and rest floating on back, tail sculling. Turn over to swim rapidly with tail and feet. Dive for abalone, crabs, urchins and mussels. Collect prey and small rock to break shells. Gregarious. Give birth to single pup at sea in June.

Kelp beds and rocky shallows with abundant shellfish, within 1 mile of shore. Alaska to California. Readily viewed off Amchitka Island, Alas. and Point Lobos, Cal. Once hunted almost to extinction for fur, now slowly increasing. Full protected.

River Otter is smaller (3ft.) and lives in fresh water. **Seals** and Sea Lions do not have hand-like forefeet.

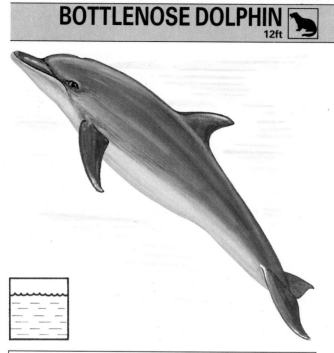

Large, robust, streamlined dolphin. Gray, darkest on back, paling to whitish pink beneath. Some have dark cape over head and sides, others spots on belly. Groove separates short beak from forehead. Crescent-shaped dorsal fin, tail fluke notched.

Use echolocation to seek prey: a variety of fish, squid, crabs and crustaceans. Follow fishing boats for discarded catch; often ride bow waves and surf. Wild dolphins occasionally approach humans. Trained to perform in dolphinaria.

In small groups in coastal waters, often in shallow bays and estuaries. Southern California to Tropics in Pacific. Most common dolphin on Atlantic coast, from Nova Scotia to Gulf of Mexico and Venezuela.

Other dolphins smaller, variously colored. Harbor Porpoise: 4–6ft.; seen in coastal waters; black back, white underside, blunt head, no beak, low dorsal fin. Alas.–S.Cal.; Greenland–N.C.

Index and check-list

All species in Roman type are illustrated
Keep a record of your sightings by checking the boxes

Abbreviations

Alas.	Alaska	**Md.**	Maryland
Arc.	Arctic	**Me.**	Maine
Bah.	Bahamas	**Mex.**	Mexico
B. Col.	British Columbia	**Mich.**	Michigan
Ber.	Bermuda	**Miss.**	Mississippi
B. Fundy	Bay of Fundy	**N.B.**	New Brunswick
Bra.	Brazil	**N.C.**	North Carolina
Cal.	California	**N.Eng**	New England
Carib.	Caribbean	**Nfld.**	Newfoundland
C. Cod	Cape Cod	**N.H.**	New Hampshire
C. Hatt	Cape Hatteras	**N.J.**	New Jersey
Ches. Bay	Chesapeake Bay	**N.S.**	Nova Scotia
Del.	Delaware	**N.Y.**	New York
Fla.	Florida	**Ore.**	Oregon
Ga.	Georgia	**Pan.**	Panama
G. Me	Gulf of Maine	**R.I.**	Rhode Island
G. Mex	Gulf of Mexico	**S.C.**	South Carolina
G. St. Law	Gulf of St. Lawrence	**Sur.**	Surinam
Ill.	Illinois	**Tex.**	Texas
La.	Louisiana	**Va.**	Virginia
L.A.	Los Angeles	**Wash.**	Washington
Lab.	Labrador	**W.I.**	West Indies
L.I.	Long Island	**Wis.**	Wisconsin
Mass.	Massachusetts	**Yuc.**	Yucatan

I.U.C.N. (1988) International Union for Conservation of Nature and Natural Resources' Red list of threatened animals (1988)

Illustrated Glossary

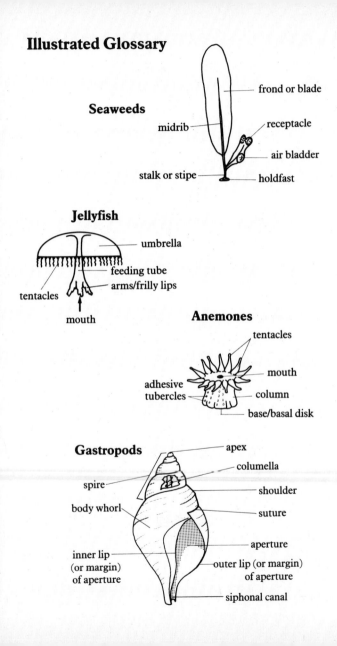

Seaweeds

frond or blade
midrib
receptacle
air bladder
stalk or stipe
holdfast

Jellyfish

umbrella
feeding tube
arms/frilly lips
tentacles
mouth

Anemones

tentacles
mouth
adhesive tubercles
column
base/basal disk

Gastropods

apex
columella
spire
shoulder
body whorl
suture
inner lip (or margin) of aperture
aperture
outer lip (or margin) of aperture
siphonal canal